Youth
BASEBALL
Drills

Peter M. Caliendo

Human Kinetics

Library of Congress Cataloging-in-Publication Data

Caliendo, Peter M.
  Youth baseball drills / Peter M. Caliendo.
      pages cm
  1. Youth league baseball--Coaching. 2. Baseball for children--Training. I. Title.
  GV880.65.C35 2014
  796.357'62--dc23
                                                2014002579
ISBN: 978-1-4504-6028-6 (print)

The web addresses cited in this text were current as of January 2014, unless otherwise noted.

Acquisitions Editor: Justin Klug; **Developmental Editor:** Anne Hall; **Assistant Editor:** Tyler M. Wolpert; **Copyeditor:** Bob Replinger; **Permissions Manager:** Martha Gullo; **Graphic Designer:** Keri Evans; **Cover Designer:** Keith Blomberg; **Photograph (cover):** © Scott Serio/Eclipse/ZUMAPRESS.com; **Art Manager:** Kelly Hendren; **Associate Art Manager:** Alan L. Wilborn; **Illustrations:** © Human Kinetics; **Printer:** United Graphics

Human Kinetics books are available at special discounts for bulk purchase. Special editions or book excerpts can also be created to specification. For details, contact the Special Sales Manager at Human Kinetics

Printed in the United States of America   10 9 8 7 6 5 4 3 2 1

The paper in this book is certified under a sustainable forestry program.

Human Kinetics
Website: www.HumanKinetics.com

United States: Human Kinetics
P.O. Box 5076
Champaign, IL 61825-5076
800-747-4457
e-mail: humank@hkusa.com

Canada: Human Kinetics
475 Devonshire Road Unit 100
Windsor, ON N8Y 2L5
800-465-7301 (in Canada only)
e-mail: info@hkcanada.com

Europe: Human Kinetics
107 Bradford Road
Stanningley
Leeds LS28 6AT, United Kingdom
+44 (0) 113 255 5665
e-mail: hk@hkeurope.com

Australia: Human Kinetics
57A Price Avenue
Lower Mitcham, South Australia 5062
08 8372 0999
e-mail: info@hkaustralia.com

New Zealand: Human Kinetics
P.O. Box 80
Torrens Park, South Australia 5062
0800 222 062
e-mail: info@hknewzealand.com

E6016

Contents

Drill Finder

Introduction

This book gives coaches quality drills that produce results and keep players energized in a successful baseball practice. It supplies coaches with drills that can be incorporated into practice plans throughout indoor and outdoor seasons.

These drills are designed to help you organize practices in a structured way so that players have the ability to improve individually but also work as a team in practice. Many of these drills will be new to you, and many will be contrary to normal baseball philosophies. The question I take into consideration when designing them is simple: If we were not already doing it this way, is this the way we would start? I don't assume there is only one way to do a drill, nor do I teach only what I was taught in the past. I always look for new, creative, and developed drills which teach the correct fundamental skills.

Philosophy

Coaching young players is a special art because we are influencing young people about how they train and play the game. If taught well, baseball training will positively influence real life experiences. Incorrect teaching methods could have dramatically negative effect on their lives as players and people.

Here are a few important questions to ask yourself as a coach:

- If you were not already doing it this way, is this the way you would start?
- As a coach what are you doing to make yourself better today?
- Did I get better today?
- Is teaching the same way as you were taught the correct approach?
- Are we practicing the players' skills during the season to maintain consistency?

After you've asked yourself those questions, you need to consider the drills themselves. As you're designing your practice plans, also keep these questions in mind:

- Is what you are teaching safe for the players?
- Can it be taught in a group practice?
- Does it accomplish good results in real time?
- Is there any testing, science, or research showing why it's done that way?

You know that you are not alone when coaching an entire team. Equipment, assistants, and support staff are all integral. Also, spend time with your coaches reviewing fundamentals and drills so everyone is on the same page. Here is a short list of the equipment and coaches you will need:

- Recruit and train good assistant coaches, both male and female.
- Clipboard to write down your practice plan.
- Wiffle balls for hitting and teaching getting away from pitches.
- Softer baseballs to help eliminate fear.
- Stopwatch to time players and your practice. Players love to be timed around the bases.
- Batting tees for stations.
- Plastic bases so you can practice on any grass or dirt. You can also set up more stations.
- Orange cones to set up lines for warm ups, area for rounding bases, and more.
- Bats, preferably light ones, so players can control it.

A whistle to help control time, signal station rotations, and let players know when to start and stop.

Coaching Myths

And finally, please think about the old rules of coaching baseball and the myths that have evolved over time. Some of these ideas are outdated, and some are downright unsafe. The following points are all ideas that should be permanently benched.

Telling players the number of outs.
Players need to think on their own. They should be asked by their coaches the number of outs or the players should tell the coaches how many there are.

Breaking in your baseball glove.
Traditionally we were all taught to take two baseballs, place them in the glove, and rap a string around the glove. The problem with this is, when you open the glove up after a couple months, it forms more of a closed glove. A better method is to turn the glove inside out when you are not using it. When you turn it back, will have a large opening which young players need.

When doing most running drills, place your glove on the bench.
Most young players should run with their glove on their hand. They need to get used to having that glove on. At times, they should also have a ball in the glove. Train how you play.

When practicing hitting, you do not have to have a helmet on.
The most obvious and important reason for having a batting helmet when hitting is for safety. Another reason is that you need to train how you play, and you play with a helmet on. This affects your head movement, balance, and more, so all the drills you do players need to have a helmet on. It does not matter if you are hitting off a tee, doing softtoss, or tossing the ball to yourself.

Young players need to use a baseball and glove when learning how to catch.

Young players should start by tossing bean bags underhand with no glove. This will teach young players to catch with two hands, and it will also reduce fear, allowing them to be successful and have fun.

Young players need to use a regular bat when learning to hit.

When learning for the first time to hit, young players need to have a wiffle bat with an oversized barrel to easily swing and make lots of contact. The coach needs to be in front of the player tossing the Wiffle ball underhand.

When you hit the ball, just run and listen for the coach.

Players need to know where the ball is so they can decide to make the turn early at first base. Players need to start early and train this way so it becomes automatic.

You must take batting practice on the field before games.

It's better to set up several stations with coaches throwing wiffles balls and players taking 5-8 swings and rotating to the next station. Players get more swings while working on on reacting to the ball.

The first baseman should roll ground balls between innings.

A more productive way would be for a coach to hit ground balls and utilize a couple players off the bench catching the ball from the first baseman. These players are alligned along the baseline as a relay team. This is more realistic and keeps more players involved. You may not be allowed to do this in some leagues, but it can be an effective tool to use in practice.

Never make the first or third out at third base.

This is a traditional rule in baseball. My question is why? Why would you not want to be aggressively intelligent? Teach your players how to be aggressive in practice and they will be that way in the game. Teaching them to not make the first or last out at third base is a defensive way to teach the game. The Anaheim Angels have an aggressive style of teaching and playing. Their results are highly acceptable. Last year, the Southern Illinois Minors, a professional independent team, were 68 of 70 when going to third in a 96 game schedule. So it can work, if implemented thoughtfully.

Use a traditional batting order.

Forget the traditional line up with a few exceptions. The leadoff hitter needs to be quick and needs to get on base. The rest of the lineup should consist of your best hitters first so they will bat more in the game. Why would I want my second hitter to be a contact guy that can run and bunt? Are you bunting in the first inning when the leadoff hitter gets on? After the first inning, you will no longer know who will be the second hitter of an inning. Why give up an out in the first inning when, with good hitters and speed, you could hit and run or steal.

Do not sacrifice bunt with two strikes.

Not true, players tend to concentrate more with two strikes. It's a good time to sacrifice bunt.

Keep batting averages.
Eliminate the batting average because it causes more problems for all hitters, especially when they hit four screamers for outs. This thinking needs to be changed to benefit the mental part of the game. More important is keeping positive at-bats by using a point system.

Coaches should tell the runner coming from first to go to third.
Start teaching your players in practice that if the ball is hit in front of them they will make the decision to go to the next base, not the third base coach. A player who has the play in front of them can make a quicker judgment because he knows his speed, sees the fielder, and can make a better decision. Players will make some wrong decisions, but overall it will make them an aggressive player who has ownership of his abilities.

When teaching pitching in the winter, always practice on a mound.
There is no reason that pitchers need to work off a mound and at full distance in the winter. They need to begin working on flat ground where there is less stress on joints, and focus on their mechanics. They can slowly begin to move back till they get back to their normal pitching distance. Finally about 3 to 4 weeks before the season begins they should begin throwing off the mound.

When practicing infield or outfield before a game, coaches should hit the first ball to the left fielder.
If you ask any baseball coach, he will tell you that he's always done it that way. This does not mean that you always have to do it this way. This only teaches players to be robots and know exactly where the ball will be hit by the coach. Other players do not even have to be ready because they know the ball will not be hit to them until it's their turn. This does not train players to be ready all the time like in a real game. By not letting the players know where the ball will go, players will be ready and react just like they should in a game.

When practicing hitting, the coach should be pitching from the mound.
You should never start your first practices with players hitting off a coach or a pitcher. First, players should be working off a batting tee to work on their swing. Then a coach should be tossing the ball to work on timing. Then, with Wiffle balls or a softer type of baseball, the coach should be about half the distance from the mound on one knee (because they are too tall for young players) throwing overhand. Keep in mind you want to eliminate fear so players can actually concentrate on their swing, balance, and vision. Once a player is confident in controlling their body, they can begin to see baseballs pitched to them at a higher speed at a further distance.

With a runner at second base, the third-base coach will help the runner.
Actually, if you have a first base coach, he has a better angle of where the shortstop is and how far the runner is from second base. Players should also learn to take their leads and be responsible for getting back or diving back to the base. They must learn how far they are from the base, look at the pitcher, and know where the fielders are by using their peripheral vision. With runners on second and third, the first-base coach will take the runner on second base.

Rules to Coach By

Now that many coaching myths have been debunked, here are some rules that should be followed when coaching. These ideas are as much about coaching in general as they are about coaching baseball specifically.

- Try and teach from the end result of a skill and work backwards. An example on hitting, place the player in a finished, balanced position and have him go backwards to his stance. As the player arrives at his stance, you can have him hit the ball off the batting tee. This teaches the hitter to load as he goes backward, the stride to time the ball, separation and more. It allows the player to understand where and how he will finish. Another example would be starting in a fielding position with a ball in the glove and then throwing.
- When teaching a skill, start as slow as possible because it's all about feel. Then as the player gets better, gradually speed up the process until you reach full speed.
- Use light objects when starting to teach the skill. For example, use a wiffle bat with an oversized barrel, build up to a broom stick, and finish with a bat.
- When the body is comfortable with the proper motion, gradually increase speed until full speed is reached.
- Train in game situations as much as possible.

Above all, remember to be positive, enthusiastic, and organized. Players feed off you, so this is very important. No one wants to have a head coach who acts like the world is ending. Stay relaxed and upbeat no matter what, and your players will have a model of good sportsmanship to guide them throughout their baseball career.

Key to Diagrams

- - - →   Ball path

Cone

Fly ball path

Ground ball

Base

Battting tee

⟶   Player movement

1

Practice Organization

Practice organization can help a coach improve the skills of individual players and prepare the team overall. If you are well organized and run a fun practice, players become better and stay in the game longer. When a player improves and shows signs of success, he will want to play the game longer.

This book cannot organize your practices for you before the season begins because we don't know the age of your players, their abilities, and the current level of their fundamentals. But we can lay down a foundation that you can follow to set up your whole plan. You establish your practice plan by considering the number of practices you have before the season begins, the ability of your players, and the equipment and facilities available.

Come Prepared for Practice

By structuring practices for competition and preparing for game situations, you can improve the success rate of your team. To run a successful practice, you need to do several things to accomplish your final goals. The following equipment will help you operate successful practices. Each section has a description of why that equipment or item is important and how it may be used.

- **Clipboard**   A clipboard gives you a place to store all your notes for practice and to write any observations that you might have about a particular player or the overall practice. Many coaches use tablets or other smart devices these days to access apps and record data at practices.
- **Batting Tees**   By setting up batting tees at stations, you can have more than one player hitting at one time. If you cannot afford batting tees, you might get someone to donate orange cones that can serve as makeshift tees.
- **Wiffle Balls**   These hollow plastic balls eliminate fear and allow players to concentrate on working on the mechanics of a swing or catching a baseball. Also, Wiffle balls do not go far when hit, so your player can get more swings when hitting. Wiffle balls can be used with any age or ability level, too.
- **Soft Baseballs**   Soft baseballs are the next stage after Wiffle balls. They also reduce fear, so players can build confidence in their mechanics. A coach can toss the ball from a kneeling position in front of a player and not fear being hit.
- **Stopwatch**   Players like to be timed. A stopwatch allows you to time runners around the bases or from base to base (from home to first, for example) and time stations so that you know when to rotate.
- **Whistle**   A whistle helps you keep the practice structured. Instead of yelling, you can blow the whistle when a certain part of practice ends and you need the players to get together with you. Use the whistle to rotate stations. When you do a team drill, you can use it as a way to say, "Go," instead of yelling it all the time.
- **Flat Bases**   You can set up flat bases in the outfield when you have several stations for throwing or fielding drills. With flat bases, you can set up a field anywhere.
- **Assistant Coaches**   Assistants allow you to have several stations so that all players are doing something all the time and no one is standing around. Volunteers

who are educated about your teaching principles, drills, and philosophy can help you keep the practice going and organized.

- **Baseball Cards**   You can use these cards as an incentive for players to listen, hustle, improve, win a game, score high on a drill, and more. You can use baseball cards when you see a player paying attention, hustling, trying to make a mechanical change, or accomplishing something positive like knowing the number of outs during the game. Cards can also be taken back when a player does something negative like not hustling, not know the number of outs, and so on. A player who sees a teammate receive a reward for a positive behavior will want to do the same thing.

- **Cones**   Cones can be used to lay out the area when you are doing warm-ups, drills, and more. Cones can signify where a player stands or where he goes during a running drill.

- **Audio Recording Device**   By having a recording device in your pocket and turning it on during practice, you will have a record of your practice session. Later you can listen to it to hear the tone of voice that you are using and what you are saying to the players. Use this recording to critique yourself and improve as a communicator.

- **Video Recording Device**   A video recording on a smart phone, tablet, or regular video recorder allows players to see and believe both what they are doing wrong and what they are doing well. To videotape players, you need to have parents fill out and sign a permission and consent form. You may want to make copies of the tapes with notes for parents so that they understand what you are trying to work on with the player.

Coaches should set up drills for players during their practices. The drills should include not only the fundamental motion used to accomplish the drill but also a competitive game. Players are more likely to do a drill with passion if it includes some kind of goal and competition. For example, if players are hitting off a batting tee, they should try to hit as many line drives as they can out of 10. Avoid having them just take 10 swings and rotate to the next station. When they do the same drill the next time, they should try to beat their previous score. When a competitive game is included with the drill, players concentrate more on the task. This translates into more learning and being able to deal with competition during a real game. Coaches should organize gamelike drills so that when players get into a real game situation, they have already been through it.

Fundamentals of Every Practice

At the end of the chapter you will see a chart that shows you how to prioritize your practices. The first part of practice should include the fundamentals that players use the most in games. They should practice these skills daily because they are the foundation of development. Then you begin looking at individual positions, such as pitching, catching, infield, and outfield. These individual positions are specialized areas that need special attention and require extra work. Last, you need to look at what your team might need to do to improve defensively, offensively, and strategically.

Hitting

Hitting is the most difficult skill for players to learn because it involves balance, vision, coordination, and timing. Young players are still developing physiologically in these areas, so you need to devote attention to detail when working with your players on hitting. Hitting is difficult at all levels but specifically at the youth level because players are still developing their physical skills. Also, because most young players select a bat that is too heavy and too long and they get too close to home plate, they develop a fear of the ball and they do not have sufficient balance while swinging the bat.

Throwing and Catching

The game is all about throwing and catching; if players cannot do this well, they will have a hard time competing as individuals or as a team. If your players can throw well, you will find it a lot easier when you need to start working on pitching. The ability to throw and catch a baseball well will enhance your team's defense and overall confidence. Coaches often assume that players know how to throw and catch a baseball, but the question is how well they can execute in a game situation. Most of the time, players play catch at a slow to average pace. They catch a baseball, look at it, grip it, and then throw it back. The other player often catches the ball one handed and goes through the same process before throwing it back. This routine can be easy because of the pace at which it is done. Players should usually catch the baseball with the bare hand near the glove so that they can transfer the ball from the glove to the bare hand quickly. If they have to reach to catch the ball, they should use one hand and bring the glove to the center of the body begin to throw the baseball.

Players often have a poor grip on the baseball, which causes them to throw incorrectly. Another thing that young players do is fail to turn the body sideways before they throw because doing so feels uncomfortable. By turning the body sideways, they can use the whole body to throw the ball.

Fielding

To reduce their fear about fielding, players need to work on fundamentals. Players who feel comfortable in their ability to field and get out of the way of a bad-hop ball will become better fielders. Their ability to react to a bad hop will increase. A major obstacle in fielding is fear of the baseball, so you should use softer baseballs when working on fielding so that the players can concentrate on technique. Players also need to learn to get into proper fielding position so that they can see the ball better. One way to work on this is to have players start in the fielding position when they field a ball so that the body is aware of the correct position at the time they field it.

Baserunning

Players run bases all the time, so they have to get good at it. This fundamental is also an instinct that needs to be practiced every day. Baserunning can also serve as your warm-up, so you do not have to waste time running laps around the field before practice. Baserunning for young players is fun because they are running, not standing around waiting, but it can be difficult to learn because it involves technique, balance, coordination, and awareness. Players often start out incorrectly from home plate. Most runners have an unbalanced swing that puts them in a poor position to run to first. So, when you are working on running to first base, have your players swing a bat, freeze at the end so that they have a balanced swing, and then start running to first. This drill helps them just drop the bat in a balanced follow-through instead of throwing it. As they run to first, many players wait until they get to first before making the turn to go to second. One way to correct this mistake is to have the hitter swing, look to see where the ball is, and, if it is past the infielders, immediately start angling toward the coach's box and start the turn early rather than late.

Bunting

Bunting can help young players improve their hitting and become more complete players. When working on bunting, start with softer baseballs, work on the technique, and then build up to using a hard baseball. After the player is confident, you can start by throwing the ball underhand and build up to throwing overhand. At a certain point you have to start throwing the ball hard to simulate game situations. Players have trouble in two areas. First is the stance. By having a good balanced stance, they gain confidence and can run after they bunt. This stance, described in the bunting chapter, has the feet in a quarter turn to home plate. Players also have a problem with gripping the bat, also described in the bunting chapter. Players who become good bunters will become better hitters because when they bunt they learn to track the ball longer. Coaches may want to have players bunt for a hit when they are struggling with their hitting.

Pitching

You should begin working on pitching as soon as you think that the players are throwing well. Pitching is where it starts and ends with a team. You need to have good pitching to compete. You should work with all young players on pitching. Instead of having just two or three pitchers, you want most of your guys to have the ability to pitch. Pitching is the most important part of the game because it all starts there. Most young players should start in a set position, not the windup. When they start in the stretch position, all they have to do is lift the leg and throw. Starting from the windup takes a lot more coordination and balance. After players learn to pitch from the stretch, accomplishing the windup is much easier. Another problem area for young pitchers is the grip of the baseball because their fingers are small. Make sure that the thumb is under the baseball and splits it. If they have to throw with a three- or four-finger grip to have better control, let them do it. Pitchers needs to learn to throw the baseball over the plate on the outside part, inside part, middle, up, and down. One way to do this is to have them aim for the catcher's knees and shoulders. These larger areas are easier for them to focus on.

Catching

Catchers are the backbone of the team. Without good catching, your pitchers will struggle, opposing teams will run more, and the dynamics of the game will change instantly. The pitcher starts the game, and the catcher is the next person who catches the ball most often in a game. So having a good catcher is important, but catchers often practice their skills only during catchers' practice, which may occur only once every two weeks, or in games. This schedule is not sufficient, and if they are practicing in games, it is too late. When playing catch, catchers should have their gear on to get used to it. During batting practice, they should be catching and working on catching the baseball at the spot where it was thrown, blocking the ball, and if you have time, coming up to throw the ball quickly back to the person who is throwing batting practice. If you have a couple of catchers, they can switch after every three hitters. Catchers need to work on three things—catching the baseball, throwing the baseball, and blocking the baseball, in that order. If they are proficient in those areas, you will have good catchers.

Position-Specific Practice Needs

When dealing with individual positions, you have only so much time at each practice. Depending on how many practices you have, you need to select exactly what areas you will work on. Players who can field and throw well can play most positions. Players then have to learn the specialized areas of their positions, which we list in the following sections. For each position, we list the top three to four areas to work on. We selected these priorities based on what the position does most often in a game.

First Base

For this specialized position, you have to teach the footwork around the base and have the player practice it so that no one gets hurt. Three skills are essential for all first basemen— working on receiving throws from all positions, working on catching balls in the dirt from all positions, and fielding ground balls.

Second Base and Shortstop

These players need to learn all the pivots and feeds on double plays. They have responsibilities on fly balls, pop-ups, steals, and special plays such as pickoffs. Communication between the shortstop and second baseman is important. They always need to know who is covering the base on a steal and who is backing up. Miscommunication can cause many problems. For example, if they both go to the bag, no one is there to take the overthrow or bad throw. Players can communicate this in many ways. A common method is for the shortstop to use an open or closed mouth, covered with the glove so that the opposition does not see it. If the shortstop has an open mouth, the second baseman takes the throw. A closed mouth by the shortstop means that the shortstop has the base and the second baseman backs it up. They need to communicate on pop-ups so that the one not catching the baseball takes or covers second base. Communication can be done in two ways, one verbally by "I got it" several times but also visually by waving the arms a few times.

Throwing to First Base and Double Plays

Throwing to first base needs to be practiced because players do that a lot in games. Make sure that they eventually do it in real game time. Turning a double play can be dangerous because a runner is coming to slide into the pivot man to prevent him from making a throw or to cause him to make a bad throw. Players can turn a double play in several ways, depending on how hard and where the ball is hit. Players must make sure to get one out first and then turn the double play.

Feeds for Double Plays

The feed, giving the baseball to the person at second base for the first out, is important. How and where the fielder throws the ball largely determines whether they can turn the double play. The technique is important. Make sure that players practice throwing from the various angles where they catch the ball. You cannot ask them to throw a baseball from a position they have not practiced. They need to practice under pressure, in real game situations, with runners and a certain time to get it done.

Third Base

The third baseman has to know where to cover on bunt situations and pop-ups. In addition, he needs to know how to start a double play. Fielding slow rollers on the run is a specialized skill that requires a lot of practice.

Throwing to First Base

As with other positions, third basemen need to learn to throw the ball from their position under game situations. At third, players throw the ball to first from various arm angles, but if you don't have enough time to practice those positions, have players always work from one position. The natural position is best. Watch them throw to determine it. Normally, it is a three-quarter throwing position.

Starting a Double Play at Second Base

To start a double play, the third baseman needs to come in slightly from his regular position. When he gets the baseball, he should stay in a good flexed position, not come up too high, and make a firm throw to second. As with all feeds, the player must look before he throws the baseball to make sure that the fielder is at the base. If he is not at the base, the player takes a shuffle with the feet toward second until he gets there.

Outfield

Outfield is the last line of defense, and the importance of the position must be communicated to your players. Some young players believe that those who play the outfield are not very good and hope that the ball will not be hit to them. Outfielders must learn to back each other up, shade the sun, and anticipate where to throw the ball.

Many of us want to work on fly balls with our outfielders. Doing this is OK, of course, if they are struggling with catching fly balls, but after they become proficient at catching them, you should hit line drives because those are the toughest plays. Teach outfielders to take a step back first with one foot and freeze for a second to get a good reading on the line drive. Start by having your outfielders practice the step and freeze without a baseball. Then you can throw baseballs to them from a short distance so that they can work on technique.

Coaches need to work on communication with the outfielders, just as they do with infield communication. Take a tennis racquet and ball and hit the ball between the outfielders. Let them work on the communication in the gaps. The center fielder normally has priority over other outfielders unless he is positioned in one gap and the ball is hit in another gap where he would have a hard time getting to it. In this case, the center fielder communicates that the other outfielder has priority. One player fields the ball, and the other backs him up on an angle, not directly in a straight line. This play also depends on how hard the ball is hit. To practice this, roll ground balls to the outfielders so that both guys move and one backs up the other. Roll it where it gets by so that the other outfielder needs to get it. Coaches need to create habits so that outfielders execute without having to think too much.

Teamwork

Finally, after you have worked on your fundamentals and individual positions, you can concentrate on teamwork. We want our players to hit the cutoff man on relays, but because they cannot throw or catch, they can accomplish neither very well. But as soon as players can execute the fundamentals, you can begin adding teamwork drills, which is a big benefit. You can mix in teamwork with the fundamentals and individual positions. As the coach, you have to decide when to do so.

Cutoffs and Relays

The game situation determines how to call a relay, when to cut it or let it go through, and what positions the players should be in. Relays can be practiced when you work on throwing. Catching and relaying a throw to another player is all about playing catch. Communication on relays is important and needs to be practiced. First, players must understand the terms and the way that you will communicate. You can then practice at a slow pace and speed up the process as the players get better.

Pickoff Plays

These plays require a lot of communication and timing, so you need to practice them a lot, not just before the season. These plays need to be executed in real game situations as well as practiced during the season. A good time to start working on this is during your catch and throw session. Pitchers can play catch together and work on pickoffs. A pickoff should be practiced in sections if young players are confused. For example, for a pickoff to first base, players must first learn to turn their feet. Then they can learn their hand position and the throw. Finally, they can do the pickoff at game speed all at once. Let your players know that they are trying to throw the ball at the level of the infielder's knees and by the base. They are trying to keep the runner close and pick him off if they can. Receivers always let the ball come to them and place the glove in front of the base that the runner is trying to get back to.

Defensive Situations With Runners on Base

You will want to practice situations that occur often in games. Prioritize the ones that you will practice by the frequency with which they happen in games, such as man on first and a ground ball, man on first and a ground ball to the outfielder, and then the same situation but a fly ball. Make sure that players know where they should throw the ball. If they do it incorrectly, practice again at a slower pace and then practice the same play live. To practice real game situations, tell your runners to go full speed and slide. You can then graduate to a man on first and a baseball hit past the outfielders. Make sure that players are proficient at this before you go on to the next thing, such as runners on first and second. At some point in your practice, you must switch up the situation to vary the pattern. Ultimately, you will have a player at home plate with a bat and baseball who tosses the ball up and hits it where he chooses. Whatever happens in the situation, players keep hitting until the team makes three outs. Then switch teams (or switch players if you do not have enough players for two teams).

Defending the Bunt

The most common situations occur when runners are on base and the opposing team is going to bunt. You need to decide how you will defend the bunt and what your signs are. As with the defensive situations described earlier, begin with the basic one—a runner on first and a sacrifice situation. This situation happens most often, so you need to work on it. Walk through what each player will do. All players yell, "Bunt" as soon as they see the hitter's hands move on the bat. Even before that, the situation may dictate a bunt, so players should remind each other what may be coming. If they do not recognize the situation, the coaches should let the players know. After the players have a good idea where to go, have a hitter bunt off a coach's pitching.

Finally, practice the play with a pitcher throwing fastballs. Then mix the pitches up if the pitcher can throw more than one pitch. The hitters decide whether they will bunt or hit. Finally, the coach gives signs to the players. If no sign is given, the players can hit away. Add your outfielders so that they are working on backing up throws. Always finish the whole play. If the ball is thrown away, play until the end. To add some fun and competition, award points if the hitter moves a runner over. Each base is a point. A successful bunt is not an out. The defense needs to get three outs before you switch defense and offense.

Defending the Steal

You will see this a lot, so your team needs to practice defending the steal. How do you hold the runner on first base? Your catcher needs to practice receiving and throwing the ball to second. You need to know the times that you need to have for the pitcher and catcher to have a chance to throw out the runner. We can simplify it and look at it this way. From the stretch, the pitcher does not want to lift his leg up high before he throws the ball. He should lift it just a few inches off the ground and a couple of inches back toward the back leg before he throws home. This action gives the runner less time to run. Before throwing home, the pitcher should throw over to first a couple of times to keep the runner close to first. These throws to home and first are simple throws. The pitcher turns around from the stretch position with both feet and gets into a position to throw to first base. The pitcher gets his body in the same position he would use to throw home, but instead he throws to first base. When the pitcher throws home, he lifts and throws home. As the ball is coming to him, the catcher starts to turn his upper body slightly, not his glove, until he catches the ball. Then he turns his feet so that he can throw to second. So these are all just catches and throws. If your team practices a lot of throwing and catching, this will all be a lot easier.

As they get better with pickoff throws, work on some finer skills to help them do it safer and quicker. Start by having no hitter, two pitchers, two catchers, two first basemen, and a second baseman and shortstop. You can also do this drill with just one at each position. The pitcher has the baseball and throws it once to first and then home. The catcher catches it and throws to second base. The shortstop or second baseman takes the throw (the other backs up the play), applies the tag, and throws the ball back to the pitcher. If you have two pitchers, as soon as the pitcher throws home he gets off the mound to get his ball back from the shortstop or second baseman. The next pitcher steps in, picks to first, and then throws home. The process continues. As the players become good at this, you can place a hitter at home so that the pitcher gets used to having a hitter in the box. As the players progress further, you can add a couple of runners at first so that they can work on diving back and stealing. If you practice this drill enough, your players will gain confidence in holding runners on and throwing them out. If the pitcher goes home and the runner does not go but is off the base, catchers should work on throwing to first base. Encourage your players not to be worried about throwing the ball away. The more they practice the pickoff, the better and more confident they will become at executing it. Give players responsibilities so they feel part of the team.

Offensive Work

Hit and runs, bunt and runs, steals, double steals, and delay steals are all part of offensive work. Create signs for these plays and decide which ones you will use more in games so that you know which ones to practice more often. Instead of having 10 offensive signs, start with the 3 or 4 signs that you will use more often and add others later if necessary. Keep it as simple as possible so that your players can remember them all. When we create complicated signs to prevent other teams from picking them up, we may confuse our own players. At the youth level, coaches should not be worried about picking up the signs of an opposing team.

Priority Chart for Practices

Table 1.1 lists the skills that you will rely on as the season progresses. Next to each item, place a checkmark to indicate that you have covered it that day. Fundamentals should be covered daily, especially hitting, playing catch, baserunning, and fielding. Pitchers and catchers need to start working together during every practice, even if they only throw at half the distance and with little speed.

Considering the number of practices, types of players, number of coaches, and type of equipment, you can prepare your outline for practices. We need to cover the fundamentals at every practice because doing so is the only way for players to get better in games. Players need to practice consistently to perfect these skills. You may decide to do less of a skill if the players are doing well in a particular area. For example, if they are throwing and catching well, decrease the time spent on those drills.

Table 1.1 Priority Chart of Skills Covered During Practices

	Monday	Tuesday	Wednesday	Thursday	Friday
Fundamental skills					
Hitting					
Throwing and catching					
Fielding					
Baserunning					
Bunting					
Pitchers' and catchers' work					
Position-specific skills					
Catchers					
Pitchers					
Outfield					
First base					
Second base and shortstop					
Third base					
Team skills					
Cutoffs and relays					
Game situations					
	Monday	Tuesday	Wednesday	Thursday	Friday
Pickoff plays					
Bunting situations					
Defensive situations					
Offensive situations					

How to Determine
Your Practice Plan

As you get into the first 5 to 10 practices, you can begin to add individual position drills. As you get more practices in, you can begin to add team skills. As you add things, you should always be considering which areas will be more important in games. I tried to prioritize topics for you in each heading, but priorities might change depending on your needs. The hardest one to prioritize is team skills. You have to determine which ones your team needs more.

Five Practices Before the Season Begins

1. All you can do here is focus all five days on throwing, fielding, pitching, catching, and hitting.

2. You teach individual skills and team skills before your games begin or during your game. For example, if the first baseman is holding the runner on first incorrectly, you can show him the correct stance between innings. If a cutoff and relay is performed incorrectly, talk about it with the players when they come off the field.

Ten Practices Before the Season Begins

1. During the first five workouts, you focus on the fundamental skills.

2. For the next five practices, you begin to add work for individual positions, such as pitcher, catcher, outfielder, and so on.

Twenty or More Practices

1. For the first five practices, focus on the fundamentals

2. For next five, decrease work on the fundamentals and start adding work for individual positions.

3. On the next five days, you can begin adding team skills. For the last five practices, add the rest of the team skills.

Practice Plans for 120 Minutes, 90 Minutes, and 60 Minutes

1. Make sure that you have your practice plan written down and placed on a clipboard.

2. With today's technology you should e-mail a practice plan ahead of time to all your players. They will then see what they are working on, how it is organized, and what to expect.

3. Make sure that you have all the equipment needed for the practice.

4. Get there early and lay out all your cones and equipment where you need it. Do not use your practice time to do this. If players are there early, have them place the items in the correct part of the field.

5. Add the sample plan that uses the drills, skills, and philosophy presented in this book.

You can use various plans. You might have stations where all players are working on the same skill but are doing different drills. For example, you could have all players working on fielding fundamentals by doing different fielding drills at each station. Or you can mix them up. You could have each of three or four stations focusing on a different fundamental. For example, you could have a hitting station, a fielding station, a throwing station, and so on.

We cannot lay out your practice for you. We offer some samples, but you have to determine what skills your players need to improve on. The important thing is to make sure that every practice includes work on throwing and catching, hitting, fielding, and baserunning. Players must practice these basic skills at every practice if they are to improve.

120-Minute Practice Plan

8:00 a.m.–8:05 a.m.	Players and coaches meet. You go over what you are looking to accomplish at that practice. Establish your expectations of players.
8:05–8:15	Team warm-up drills
8:15–8:45	Station 1: Team throwing and catching drills
	Station 2: Team fielding and throwing drills
	Station 3: Rundown drills
	Rotation among stations after 10 minutes
8:45–8:50	Water break
8:50–9:30	Station 1: Team sliding drills
	Station 2: Team hitting drills
	Station 3: Team baserunning drills
9:30–9:35	Water break
9:35–10:00	Individual positions

90-Minute Practice Plan (Example 1)

8:00 a.m.–8:05 a.m.	Players and coaches meet. You go over what you are looking to accomplish at that practice. Establish your expectations of players.
8:05–8:15	Team warm-up drills
8:15–8:30	Team throwing and catching drills
8:30–8:45	Team fielding and throwing drills
8:45–8:55	Team sliding drills
8:55–9:05	Rundown drills
9:05–9:30	Team hitting drills

90-Minute Practice Plan (Example 2)

8:00 a.m.–8:05 a.m.	Players and coaches meet. You go over what you are looking to accomplish at that practice. Establish your expectations of players.
8:05–8:15	Team warm-up drills
8:15–8:45	Station 1: Team throwing and catching drills
	Station 2: Team fielding and throwing drills
	Station 3: Rundown drills
	Rotation among stations after 10 minutes
8:45–8:50	Water break
8:50–9:30	Station 1: Team sliding drills
	Station 2: Team hitting drills
	Station 3: Team baserunning drills

60-Minute Practice Plan

8:00 a.m.–8:05 a.m.	Players and coaches meet. You go over what you are looking to accomplish at that practice. Establish your expectations of players.
8:05–8:15	Team warm-up drills
8:15–8:30	Team throwing, catching, and fielding drills all at one time
8:30–9:00	Hitting game

2

Warm-Up Drills

These warm-ups account for the limited time you have for practice. The objective is to do warm-ups that both warm up the body and work on specific skills of the game so that you do not waste time having players run around the field a few times to get warmed up. Running around the field accomplishes only one thing, warming up, and the activity is boring for young players. These exercises are done first in your practice and do not take a long time. You can add or subtract exercises depending on the time that you have for practice. Warms-ups do not need to take more than 5 to 10 minutes, but they must be productive.

Try to keep the listed sequence of the warm-ups because the specific order will help players stretch and run.

1. Jump in Place and Go

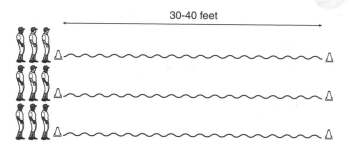

30-40 feet

Purpose

To have players work on developing stronger legs and exploding to a run. The explosion helps develop the lower body.

Equipment

Cones   Baseball for each player
Glove for each player

Number of Players

Full team

Setup

Have the players line up in several lines, each with his fielding glove and a baseball.

Procedure

1. Players begin to jump as high as possible by jumping and bringing their knees up.
2. They continue to do this until you blow the whistle. They then jog to the next cone.
3. When one line starts jogging forward and there is enough room so that the players will not interfere with the other players, whistle for the next line to go.
4. To keep the drill running smoothly and quickly, do not wait long to whistle the next time.

Coaching Points

-   Make sure that the players are bringing their knees up as high as possible. They should not stop doing this until you blow the whistle. They then begin to run.
-   Watch that they keep their arms close to their bodies as they throw their hands up with their knees to create more power going up.

Variation

A challenging variation is for players to jump one time off the right leg and one time off the left leg, instead of using both legs.

2. Strides Forward

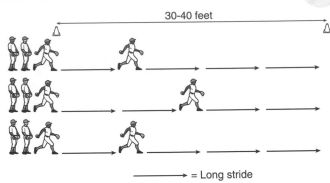

➙ = Long stride

Purpose

To stretch and strengthen the lower part of the body and work on balance and flexibility. By working on this drill, the players are also working on getting the body into better backhand and forehand fielding positions. The drill works on players' balance, which helps them with the skills of throwing, fielding, and pitching.

Equipment

Two cones   Baseball for each player

Glove for each player

Number of Players

Full team

Setup

Have players line up in several lines, one behind another with their gloves on and each with a baseball in his glove.

Procedure

1. Blow the whistle to tell the first line to stride forward with the right foot as far as possible as long as they can keep their balance. They then stride forward with the left foot and continue alternating feet until they reach the next cone.

2. When the first line gets ahead sufficiently, blow the whistle. This continues until everyone gets to the end. To prevent players from getting bored, do not wait long to blow the whistle for the next group.

Coaching Points

- Watch for players who do not take a long stride and fail to drop the knee close to the ground.
- Watch for players who overstride and are off balance, although this does not occur as often.

Variations

As players stride out with the right foot, they can turn and stretch to the left side. Another variation is for players to place the elbow on the striding side as low as possible to the outside of the striding leg, close to the ground.

3. Running in Place and Run

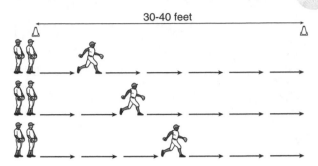

Purpose
To develop quick feet and explosive movements forward. Running in place helps players run on the balls of their feet, works their arm pump close to the body, and conditions them at the same time.

Equipment
Two cones

Glove for each player

Baseball for each player

Number of Players
Full team

Setup
Line up players in several lines, one behind another.

Procedure
1. When you blow the whistle, players in the first line, with their fielding gloves on and with a baseball in the glove or throwing hand, begin to move their feet up and down as fast as possible. They keep their feet low to the ground and develop short, choppy steps.
2. When you blow the whistle, the first line starts running forward to the next cone at a pace a little quicker than a jog.
3. Blow the whistle to start the next group and continue until everyone reaches the other side. Players do it again going back.

Coaching Points
- Players should keep the knees bent.
- The hands should be to the side of the body, not away from it.
- Players should be flexed at the waist and in a good athletic position.
- The feet should be slightly wider than the shoulders.

4. Shuffles

30-40 feet

Purpose

To work on quick side-to-side movement to help players understand how to use the body to throw the ball. Players need to understand that after they catch a baseball, they need to move forward and turn sideways before they throw it.

Equipment

Two cones   Baseball for each player

Glove for each player

Number of Players

Full team

Setup

Line up players in several lines, one behind another with their gloves and each with a baseball.

Procedure

1. The first line of players turns sideways so that the glove shoulder points to the cone that they will shuffle to as soon as you blow the whistle. Make sure that they are gripping the baseball and that the baseball is in the glove at waist level.

2. On your whistle, the first line begins to shuffle with a ball in the hand and both the hand and the ball in the glove at about chest level. The elbows should be down.

3. As the players shuffle their feet, make sure that their feet do not touch and that they do not jump.

4. After all of them reach the other end, the process begins again going the other way. Make sure that the glove shoulder is always turned toward the area that they are shuffling to.

Coaching Points

- Look for players who are bouncing as they shuffle. They need to stay flexed at the knees and keep the feet low to the ground.
- Make sure that players do not touch their feet when they shuffle.
- The head should be straight ahead so that they know where they are going.
- When they are shuffling, the back leg should not go behind the front one because then the momentum is going in another direction.
- If they do not have a good grip on the baseball or the player whom they are throwing to is not looking or has not yet reached the base, they should shuffle until they are ready to throw.

Variations

To perform this variation, players shuffle until they hear a whistle. They then run. When they hear the whistle again, they shuffle again. This drill can develop good footwork as the players warm up. Another variation is to have players run backward by leaning forward. When they hear the whistle, they turn and run forward. When they hear the whistle again, they run backward. They do this several times until they reach the next cone.

5. Hitting Position and Run

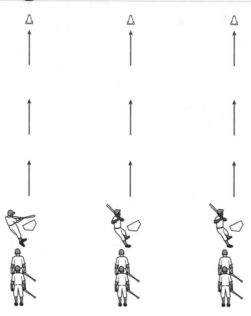

Purpose

This warm-up drills works on several things—the swing, balance, the back foot stepping to first base, and running. It teaches players what the next step is after the swing so that they do not waste any time.

Equipment

Three bases

Three cones

Bat for each player

Three home plates (optional)

Number of Players

Full team

Setup

Line up players in several lines, one behind another. Each player holds a bat by the barrel, for safety reasons. Players are less likely to swing a bat in line if they hold it by the barrel rather than by the grip. When a player's turn comes, he grabs the bat by the grip and gets ready. Also, make sure that players are some distance apart so that they are not hit with a bat. Players in the first line get into hitting position, slightly turned so that after they swing they are in position to run to first base, just as they would at a regular field.

Procedure

1. On your whistle, the players in the first line swing and freeze. On the second whistle, they drop the bat. On the third whistle, they run by taking the back foot and bringing it directly to the base or area that they are running to.

2. If you have home plates, place one by each hitter. This drill can be done without home plates.

3. Have the players practice running through the base placed at the end of the line where the cone is located,

4. After the first line of players swings the bat and begins to run, the next group gets ready and you blow the whistle again.

Coaching Points

- Make sure that the players are lined up properly by home plate and have a good balanced stance.

- As they swing, they need to freeze when they finish the swing. At first they do not have to swing fast. Have them do it slowly to warm up and to understand the swing. As they get better, they can speed up the swing to a maximum swing.

- When they freeze, make sure that they are completely balanced because a balanced position will correct many problems in the mechanics of the swing.

- As they begin to run, the back foot should go directly forward to first base so that they do not waste any time and run in a straight line.

- Make sure that they run through first base and do not stop on or slow down at the base. They should touch the front part of the base. After they pass the base, they should lower the center of gravity, spread the feet to slow down, and turn the head to the right to see whether the ball was overthrown.

Variation

You can have a coach by a base at the end of the run throw a ball in the direction of an overthrow to see whether the runner sees the ball. If the player sees the ball, he pushes off with the foot closer to the base and takes a couple of steps as if he is going to second base. Have a player off to the side chasing down the overthrows so you don't lose time going after them.

6. Right, Left, Field

30-40 feet

Purpose
To work on fielding position, stretch the body out, and get the muscles used to the fielding position.

Equipment
Two cones

Glove for each player

Baseball for each player

Number of Players
Full team

Setup
Line up players in several lines, one behind another with their gloves and each with a baseball in his glove.

Procedure
1. The players in the first line practice moving their feet as they get into ready position. When you blow the whistle, right-handed throwers take a short right step forward and left-handed throwers take a short step with the left foot. The next short step with the opposite foot is to the side to widen the base. Players then bend the knees and lower the fingertips of the glove to the ground. The bare hand is either to the side of the glove or on top of it as the players go into the fielding position. So it's right, left, field (for a right-hander).
2. They keep doing this until they get to the last cone.
3. Players do this drill slowly and under control. It is not a race. They have a ball in the glove when doing the drill.
4. In this drill they are simulating the fielding position.
5. As they do this drill, they develop flexibility because they are stretching the body. At the same time, they develop some strength.

Variation
Players can do the same drill and simulate the backhand or the forehand.

7. Fundamental Skills, Warm-Up, and Stretch

Purpose

This drill is designed to work on all the fundamentals skills while players are stretching out the body. It works on throwing, fielding, hitting, and sliding.

Equipment

Baseball and glove for each player

Number of Players

Full team

Setup

All players are in a circle, and the coach is at one end where all players can see him. Each player has his glove on with a baseball in it.

Procedure

1. You begin by yelling out a position. The players then get into that position.
2. Here are some examples: fielding position, throwing position, throw, hitting position, contact position, finish, freeze, sliding position.

Coaching Points

- Start slowly so that the players understand the positions.
- Be sure that they are going into those positions and transitioning into the next skill.
- As the players improve, increase the speed to add some intensity.
- Eventually you will not need to demonstrate the skills anymore; you can simply call them out by name. Stay consistent with the names of the skills.
- When they become proficient, have a different player be the leader each day. The leader calls out the skills and demonstrates them.
- This drill should not take long. Two or three minutes are all that is needed.

8. Strides Backward

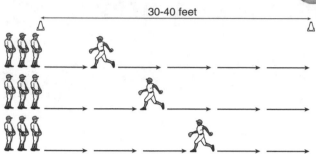

Purpose

To stretch and strengthen the lower part of the body. Along with working on balance and flexibility, this drill works on players' balance, which helps them with the skills of throwing, fielding, and pitching.

Equipment

Two cones   Baseball for each player

Glove for each player

Number of Players

Full team

Setup

Line up players in several lines, one behind another. They have their gloves, and each has a baseball.

Procedure

1. On your whistle, players in the first line, with their fielding gloves on and a baseball in the hand or glove, begin to stride backward with the right foot as far as possible, then with the left, and then with right, alternating feet until they reach the next cone.

2. On your whistle, the next line goes. Keep doing this until everyone gets to the other side.

3. This process continues from one end to the other. To keep players from becoming bored, blow the whistle as soon as there is enough room for the next line to go. You want to keep players going all the time.

Coaching Points

- Watch for players who do not take a good long stride and do not drop the knee close to the ground.
- Watch for players who overstride and are off balance, although this does not occur as often.
- This drill will be much harder than Strides Forward, so you may have to practice it more.
- When players stride, they need to feel the legs stretch and stride as far as they can while staying balanced and under control.
- Most players are not strong and flexible in the lower body, so they take a short stride in all the skills, which causes major problems in trying to accomplish the fundamentals.

9. Going After Fly Balls

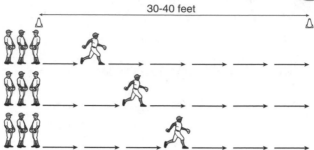

Purpose

This drill allows players to work on their ability to go after ground balls or fly balls. It can also help with angles on balls and getting to a ball faster than by using the old-fashioned method of dropping back with a foot and crossing over.

Equipment

Two cones

Glove for each player

Baseball for each player

Number of Players

Full team

Setup

Line up players in several lines, one behind another with their gloves and each with a baseball.

Procedure

1. The players in the first line have their backs to the cone that they are going to run to.
2. When you blow the whistle, they turn their hips quickly to the right side, which puts them in a position to run. As their hips turn and their feet land on the ground, they push off with the back leg and run past the cone.
3. As soon as the first group takes off, the second group gets ready and you blow the whistle.
4. When all groups are done, they come back the other way on your whistle and turn over the left shoulder. They will be weaker in turning to one side, and they need to work hard on getting better on that side.

Coaching Points

- Be sure that the players do not jump straight up as they develop the hip turn.
- Make sure that as they turn, they stay flexed at the knees and keep their feet low to the ground.
- As they turn, they should gain some ground toward the area that they are going to run to and not turn in the spot where they started.
- As they run, they pretend to look at a ball in the air.

Variation

To make this drill more gamelike, use several lines and have a coach at each line. After the player turns and runs, the coach throws him a baseball, which the player catches on the run.

3

Throwing and Catching Drills

The skill of throwing and catching a baseball is difficult for young players to accomplish. Many players have a fear of the ball, which is a natural thought process, and after they get hit by the ball, the fear may become even more real. One thing that coaches can say to ruin their credibility with young players is, "Come on. That ball doesn't hurt." If I were a young player, I would ask the coach whether I could throw the ball at him to see whether it hurts. At the same time, to have confidence in their ability to throw and catch a baseball, players have to become confident in their technique first.

Glove Care and Size

As for receiving the baseball, we need to make sure that players do a few things technique wise to build their confidence. First, the player's glove is extremely important. It is not about how much a glove costs; it's about how it is broken in and maintained throughout the year. Many of us, including me, were taught to break in a glove by putting a baseball in it, tying a string around it, and keeping it like that in the off-season. The problem is that the glove forms into a closed position, and a young player may not be able to open it up with his hand. So instead of breaking in the glove the old way, players should try a new way. They should turn the glove inside out and leave it like that when they do not use it. Players should not use a big glove because then they just reach out and hope that the ball lands in it. You want young players to have a small glove that forces them to use two hands. They can get the ball out easier, and they have to move to the baseball with their feet rather than reach out with an oversized glove.

Ball Size

Many young players have to grip the ball with three fingers across the seam or even four because their hands are too small to hold the ball properly. The Japanese have gone to a smaller baseball for young players so that they can grip it and throw it correctly. Later they build up to throwing a regulation-size baseball. This approach is a good way to teach young players to throw the ball correctly. In the United States, people are against it because they believe that using a small ball is not real baseball. We need more coaches who think outside the box when it comes to developing young players. Most of us tend to teach the way that we were taught, and most of the time that is the same old way of traditional teaching.

Receiving Position

Players who set up in proper receiving position will gain the confidence to stay in the right position or get out of the way if for some reason someone throws the ball to them and the sun gets in their eyes. We used to teach players not to throw the ball unless the receiver was looking at them and his hands were out in front. We still do this, but we now teach different hand positioning. The old way was to have the thumbs of the glove and the bare hand together and the fingertips facing up to the sky. Because of this teaching and because players often used big gloves, many players, as the ball got closer to them, had to flip the palm of the glove to the sky to see the ball. The ball would sometimes hit the heel of the glove and then hit them in the head. To make sure that they can see the ball as it is on the way, which will allow them to use their depth perception, we now start the hands and the glove with the thumbs up to the sky and the hands out in front. The player is in a good balanced position. The feet are about shoulder-width apart, and the right foot is slightly behind the left (opposite for left-handed throwers). The toes of the rear foot should be about even with the instep of the other foot.

Receiving to Throwing Position

As the player receives, the ball he takes the glove and brings it to his hand at the center of his body. As the glove and hand come together, the transfer of the baseball from the glove to the hand begins. As this occurs the body begins to turn completely sideways so that the glove-side shoulder points directly to the target. The player can then use his entire body to throw the ball. You can show players why they want to turn sideways by having them sit down and throw the ball. Then have them stand up, turn sideways, and throw the baseball. They will be able to throw it farther and straighter by standing up sideways. This experiment will prove it to them right away. By turning sideways they can also move toward the target to gain momentum, get closer to the target, and move the elbows of both arms as high as their shoulders. As they begin to turn the body sideways and grip the baseball, they will begin to drop their hands in a circular motion and then move them back up as the elbows lift the hands even with the shoulders. The arms should be in a 90-degree angle mirroring each other. This should occur before the glove-side foot touches the ground completely. This phase of gaining ground as they begin to turn the body sideways is important for young players. They will begin to understand that this positioning will allow them to rotate faster and throw the baseball harder.

In this chapter we show you drills that can be done in sequence during practices and before games. By staying consistent with drills that help improve players' throwing and receiving, you will see improvement in your team's defensive performance. Players need to work on throwing and catching a baseball daily to improve at a good pace. Practicing 15 minutes a day for 6 or 7 days is better than practicing for more than an hour once per week.

> When a player throws the ball so that the receiver cannot catch it, even when he moves, have the player who threw the baseball retrieve it. The receiver takes the spot of the player who threw the ball. This approach encourages players to focus more on what they are doing.

When you do the drills as a team, you should yell out commands such as "Ready" and "Throw." This method encourages discipline, consistency, and teamwork, and you can see everyone at one time instead of trying to watch players as they are doing the drills on their own. In addition, players tend to work hard to make each other look good. The receiver moves faster to try to get the baseball.

Teach players always to anticipate bad throws so that they are ready to move quickly. If a player going after a bad throw does not sprint after the ball to get back in line, continue to do the drill with the group.

Do not wait for a player to retrieve the ball and get back in line. You need to say, "Ready" loudly to the group (or use a whistle). The player not hustling after the ball will then sprint because he does not want to miss the next drill or throw with the group. As the players improve at their drills, you can change the speed of your voice. After you say, "Ready," you then quickly say, "Throw." As soon as the other players receive the ball, you yell, "Ready" right away so that the players hurry to their ready position. The players will follow the speed of your voice.

To work on the players' listening skills, you can use different words to mean "throw," like "red," "car," and "now."

The following drills are designed for coaches who do not have many practices before the season, but all coaches can use them. For these drills, especially with really young players, color all your baseballs one color on one side and leave the other side white. You may want to use your team color on the baseballs. You want to split the ball in half with the color by drawing a line directly around the ball straight through the four seams. The idea here is that when the player grips the ball correctly and throws it correctly, the colors stay on the side. If the color gets on top or on an angle, the player is doing something wrong with his mechanics or grip. In these drills make sure that the players are always throwing the ball on a straight line or in a downward plane, never up. They should always take the head, eyes, and body toward the target. The drills have been set up from a backward sequence, from the end to the start of the throwing motion. This pattern helps players understand where they need to be in all the sequences of their body movement. By starting with the release, they know where they should be when they release the baseball. Most players do not know or have never felt that position, so they release the ball where they have always released it, most likely too early. The result is high throws.

10. Throwing Grip

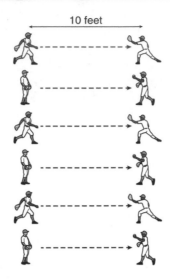

10 feet

Purpose

Throwing the baseball correctly is vital to the success and safety of individual players and the team. For young players several things must happen when throwing a baseball. First, they must have a proper grip. A baseball has four horseshoe, or C, seams. Players should grip the ball with two fingers across the C seams so that they are throwing a four-seam fastball. This grip allows a ball thrown from an upward to a downward angle to travel straight and fast. Players should practice this grip each time they catch the baseball and transfer it from the glove to the throwing hand. They feel for the seams as the transfer occurs. The more they practice getting the correct grip, the more of a habit it becomes and the better they get at it. This type of grip allows a good backspin to the baseball and uses the four seams as they rotate to take the air particles on top of the ball and place them underneath it, thus keeping the ball going straight longer. If the air particles are on the side of the ball, the ball moves right or left. This movement is not productive when the player is throwing to a base to get the runner out or performing a relay throw. Players want to keep the ball straight and low so that it travels to the target quicker.

Equipment

Baseballs

Number of Players

Full team

Setup

Place same number players on each side as if they are playing catch. How far apart they are depends on their age and their skill at doing the drill.

Procedure

1. Each player on one side has a baseball. Have the partners close to each other on this drill when they start.
2. On your whistle, the players with the baseballs toss the ball underhand to their partners.
3. The players receiving the ball catch it, bring it straight up, and show the grip. They see how good their grip is from catching to transfer.
4. On your whistle, throwing and catching continues back and forth.

Coaching Points

- The most important point for young players is putting the thumb in the right spot as they grip the baseball.
- They should place the thumb directly underneath the baseball so that it splits the ball in half. This grip of the ball keeps the ball balanced in the hand as the player releases it.
- If the player places the thumb to the side of the ball, as many players do, the thumb pushes the ball out to the side.
- Everything in the mechanics of the throwing motion can be correct, but if the ball slips out of the hand at the last moment on release, it will travel in the wrong direction.

11. Wrist and Arm

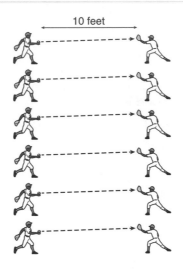

10 feet

Purpose

This drill isolates the last actions of the throwing motion, taken with the wrist. The drill takes away the rest of the body so that the player can concentrate on the proper position and movement of the wrist.

Equipment

Baseball colored in half for each group playing catch

Number of Players

Full team

Setup

Line up the players into two lines with the same number players on each side, 10 feet apart. Players face each other, and their toes and chest face the target. The players with the baseball grip the ball correctly and place the throwing arm in a 90-degree angle with the elbow even with the shoulder. They do not rotate or use the lower to upper body, just the wrist and arm. Their glove should be in front of their chest with the inside part facing toward their chest.

Procedure

1. On your whistle, the players with the ball flick the ball with the wrist to their partners.
2. The receiving player, in a good ready position, receives the ball. As soon as the ball hits the glove, he takes it out quickly and gets to the 90-degree angle.
3. Throwing continues back and forth on your whistle for 5 to 10 throws per player.

Coaching Points

- Make sure that players start in a good athletic position when throwing and receiving the baseball.
- The player throwing the ball should have the hand behind the baseball, not to the side.
- As he flicks the wrist to throw the ball, the player keeps the fingers behind it so that the ball goes straight.
- The player throwing the ball should have the wrist go forward, not to one side.
- The receiver looks for the transfer and the 90-degree angle that the arm gets into after the transfer.

12. Wrist Stride

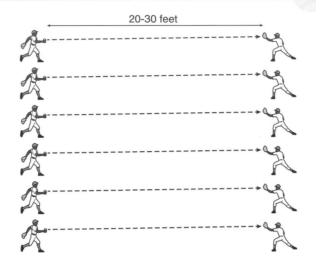

20-30 feet

Purpose

The second phase of the throwing motion is important because it begins to work with balance and velocity. In this drill players use the wrist, arm, and chest to throw.

Equipment

Baseball colored in half for each group playing catch

Number of Players

Full team

Setup

Place players facing each other and farther apart than they were in the previous drill. Players with the baseball have the stride foot forward and grip the ball correctly, placing the throwing arm in a 90-degree angle, elbow even with the shoulder. Throw the baseball by taking the head, eyes, chest, arm, and wrist forward.

Procedure

1. On your whistle, the players with the ball throw it to their partners.
2. As soon as the ball hits the receiving player's glove, he takes it out quickly and gets to the 90-degree angle, with the stride foot forward.
3. Throwing continues back and forth on your whistle for 5 to 10 throws.

Coaching Points

- When you yell, "Ready," make sure that players are in proper position.
- The player throwing the ball should have the hand behind the baseball, not to the side. Make sure that players use the whole upper body to go forward to release the baseball so that the back leg comes up and forward. When players throw the ball, the wrist should go forward, not to one side.

13. Toss-Up Grip

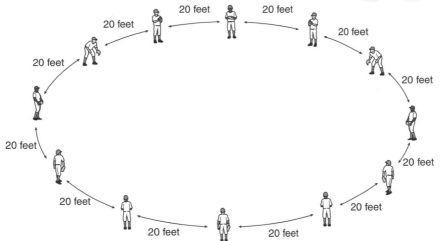

Purpose

Players can practice this grip by tossing the ball up, catching it, and getting the proper grip as they simulate a throw. Getting the proper grip in a game will become second nature after performing this drill consistently. The important thing is to have the thumb underneath the baseball to keep it firm and balanced in the hand.

Equipment

Baseball for each player

Number of Players

Full team

Setup

Give each player a baseball and put them in a circle with about 20 feet between each player.

Procedure

1. When you blow the whistle, the players toss the ball up and catch it.
2. As they catch it, they transfer the baseball from the glove to the hand and try to come up with a good grip. When you blow the whistle again, the process continues.

Coaching Points

-   At the start of this drill, have the players toss the ball up and slowly take the ball out of the glove. They work on the feel of how to get a good grip.
-   As they improve, have them pick up the speed and see whether they can still get the proper grip.
-   When they get good at this, have them take the ball out and get the correct grip as they get into a throwing position.

14. Fear of the Baseball

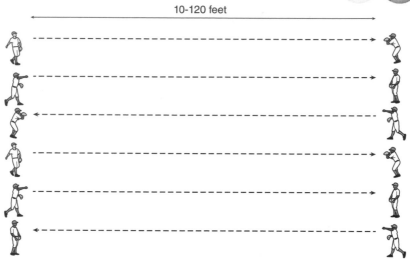

10-120 feet

Purpose

If players fear the baseball or lack the skill to catch it, start with a simpler concept. Use beanbags, tennis balls, or softer baseballs and have them work on catching the ball thrown underhand with no glove. This drill helps players understand (all players should start this way) how the hands work together when catching the baseball. When the hands understand how to catch, catching it will be much easier when the glove is on the hand. This drill is fun, and they will get much better at it as they do it more often.

Equipment

A softer baseball or beanbag for each player

Number of Players

Full team

Setup

Place the same number players on each side as if they are playing catch.

Procedure

1. Have all the players toss the beanbag, tennis ball, or softer ball up to themselves and catch it with two hands. The players now know exactly how high to throw the ball. As they get better, they will toss it a little higher, eventually tossing it high as a challenge.

2. Players then toss the ball underhand to each other.

3. You can also have players toss the ball underhand to each other and catch it with either hand. This one-hand drill teaches kids to use both hands at a young age. You may not be sure which hand the very young age players catch and throw with.

4. To make it more fun, you can have lines of players shuffling their feet as they toss the ball underhand back and forth. They can do this for 40 feet, turn around the other way, and go back. They would do this after they become proficient at catching the underhand toss from each other without moving. This progression adds an element of fun and skill development.

Coaching Points

- When receiving the ball, players step to the throw depending on where the throw is, and they gain ground when catching the baseball. They then throw after they catch it.

- When receiving the baseball, players should have the hands to the side and out in front. The thumbs face the sky.

- When the ball is thrown to the right or left, players want to push off with the right foot if going left and the left foot if going right. Most players pivot their feet to receive the baseball, which is a much slower movement because as they pivot they create friction with their feet against the ground.

- Then, after they push off, they turn sideways and throw. The push-off gives them momentum in that direction. As they run for the ball, they determine whether they can get in front of it or have to catch it by reaching out. This will depend on where they are relative to the flight and velocity of the baseball.

- Players should not try to reach with both the glove and the hand when they cannot get in front of the ball. Doing this does not allow the glove hand to go as far as it can by reaching out only with the glove hand. Coaches sometimes require players always to get in front of the ball, which may cause them to be caught in the wrong position to catch the baseball. Coaches want players to move their feet, so they tell them to get in front of all balls, but they need to start teaching kids to reach for the balls at times to the forehand and backhand. When players practice this skill, they improve significantly.

15. Rotated-T Position

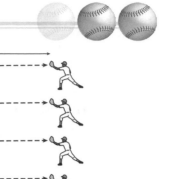

30 feet

Purpose

This drill is another step back from the first two drills. You continue to work the fundamental skill backward and then go forward. The players know how to get there because they have been there in the first two drills.

Equipment

Baseball colored in half for each group playing catch

Number of Players

Full team

Setup

Line up the players with partners. Move them farther apart than they were in the previous drill because the ball travels faster in this drill. Players face each other, and the players with the baseball have the stride foot forward and the upper body turned to the side. The players with the baseball grip the ball correctly and place the throwing arm in a 90-degree angle with the elbow even with the shoulder and the arms parallel to the group. They do not rotate or use the lower to upper body but throw the baseball by taking the head, eyes, chest, arm, and wrist forward.

Procedure

1. On your whistle, the players with the ball throw it to their partners by rotating the upper body like a Ferris wheel.

2. The receiving player, in a good ready position, receives the ball. As soon as the ball hits the glove, he takes the ball out quickly and gets to the 90-degree angle. He then gets in a position with the stride foot forward and throws on your whistle.

3. Throwing continues back and forth on your whistle for 5 to 10 throws per player.

Coaching Points

- When you yell, "Ready," the players get in the proper position so that you can see that everyone is in the correct position before you blow the whistle.

- The player throwing the ball should have the hand behind the baseball, not to the side.

- In this drill, make sure that players start with the upper body rotated back to the side, not with the chest facing their partner.

- Make sure that they use the whole upper body to go forward to release the baseball so that the back leg comes up and forward.

- Look for the player throwing the baseball to rotate the upper body like a Ferris wheel, not a merry-go-round.

- When players receive the ball, look for the transfer and the 90-degree angle that the arm gets into after the transfer.

Variations

Have players do the same drill but now cross their arms as if they are hugging themselves. They lift the front leg to keep rhythm and throw. This variation helps players relax their arms and not be too stiff. Players can then add stepping with the back foot behind and forward on the other foot. As they do this, they cross their arms and lift the front foot, which creates a torque that allows the body to throw the ball harder. Emphasize to the players that this is the only time they step behind the front foot when throwing, to work on slightly closing the front hip. Also, in both variations, when they hug themselves with the arms (cross them in a 90-degree angle), the hand with the ball comes over the glove hand so that the baseball and elbow get up to the throwing position quicker.

16. Sideways Position With Hands Together

40 feet

Purpose

The purpose of this drill is to put players in a sideways position that they have to get to any time they catch a baseball or grounder. This drill cuts down the direction of the throw, gives players rhythm to throw, and allows them time to get the elbows even with the shoulder when they throw.

Equipment

Baseball colored in half for each group playing catch

Number of Players

Full team

Setup

Line up the team with the same number players on each side. Move them farther apart than they were in the previous drill because the ball will travel faster in this drill. Players receiving the ball are in a receiving position, and players throwing the ball begin sideways, ready to shuffle and throw.

Procedure

1. On your whistle, the players with the ball shuffle and throw the baseball to their partners. As they shuffle, their hands come down in a circular motion and the elbows rise to shoulder level. They do this in one smooth motion with rhythm.

2. The receiving player, in a good ready position, receives the ball. As soon as the ball hits his glove, he takes it out quickly and gets to a throwing position, turned sideways with the elbows at shoulder level and the arms in a 90-degree angle. After he gets to this position, you whistle. He places his hands together and gets into a sideways position ready to throw on the next whistle.

3. Throwing continues back and forth on your whistle for 5 to 10 throws per player.

Coaching Points

- When you yell, "Ready," the players get in the proper position so that you can see that everyone is in the correct position before you blow the whistle.

- When players are throwing the ball, make sure that they are turned completely sideways. This mistake is common because players think that they are completely turned when they are not. They have to feel the exact position.

- Look for the players throwing the baseball to shuffle by bringing their feet close together but not touching. The upper body should rotate like a Ferris wheel, not a merry-go-round.

- As the players rotate to throw after the shuffle, watch that they do not rotate the upper body too early. As late as possible is better, and the head and chest should go toward the glove.

- When players receive the ball, look for the transfer of the baseball and see that they get to the throwing position quickly.

Variation

Instead of shuffling and throwing the baseball, the players can take the back foot (the right foot for a right-handed thrower) and step over the front foot before throwing the baseball. Some people call this a crow hop, but you want to make sure that the back foot goes directly over the front foot, not up and over.

17. Ball in Glove

50 feet

Purpose

This drill teaches players how to throw the ball after it is caught in any direction. It trains players how to right their position in preparation to throw after an awkward catch.

Equipment

Baseball colored in half for each group playing catch

Number of Players

Full team

Setup

Line up the players with partners and move them back from the position they took in the previous drill because the ball will travel faster in this drill. Players receiving the ball are in a receiving position, and players throwing the ball begin with the glove in front, the ball in the glove, and their toes and chest facing the receiver.

Procedure

1. On your whistle, the players with the ball begin to move forward with the back leg (the right leg for right-handed throwers and the left for left-handers). As they move forward, they work on transferring the baseball from the glove to the hand and throwing. As they move forward, they begin to come down in a circular motion as the elbows rise to shoulder level. They do this all in one smooth motion with rhythm.

2. The receiving player, in a good ready position, receives the ball. As soon as the ball hits the glove, he takes the ball out quickly and gets to a throwing position, turned sideways with the elbows at shoulder level and the arms at a 90-degree angle. After he gets to this position, you whistle, and he goes back to the starting position. This sequence assures that players are always working on transferring the baseball, a key area in throwing.

3. This continues back and forth on your whistle for 5 to 10 throws per player.

Coaching Points

- When you yell, "Ready," the players get in proper position so that you can see that everyone is in the correct position before you blow the whistle.

- Make sure that the players throwing the ball are turned completely sideways and are moving forward to the target. This mistake is common because players think that they are completely turned when they are not. They have to feel the exact position and feel their bodies going forward. They can then use the whole body and momentum to throw the baseball with authority.

- Look for the players throwing the baseball to move forward, turn, and throw. The upper body should rotate like a Ferris wheel as they throw the baseball.

- As the players with the ball rotate to throw after they move forward, look that they do not rotate the upper body too early. The rotation should come as late as possible, and the head and chest should go toward the glove.

- The receiver should transfer the baseball and get to the throwing position quickly.

Variation

Players can begin with the ball in the glove anywhere in front of them, above their head, to the side—simulating any kind of throw.

18. Fielding Position and Throw

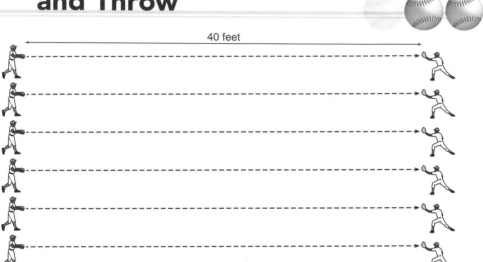

40 feet

Purpose

This drill works on three things. It puts the player in a fielding position so that he bends his knees and gets his glove out in front with his bare hand near the glove. From this position, he throws to his partner by again taking his back foot forward, gaining ground toward the target, building momentum going forward, and throwing the baseball. Every time a player gets into this fielding position, he is developing his muscles and neuromuscular system to understand that position. Doing this is difficult for young players because they have never been in that spot. Performing this drill strengthens the muscles and makes them more flexible, helping players get into fielding position more easily. The drill also eliminates the players' fear of the ball coming at them (because the ball is already in the glove) and allows them to focus on the individual fundamental skill of the fielding position. The drill teaches players that as they move forward to throw the baseball, they need to pick up the head, pick up the target, and throw the baseball. Many players field and begin to throw before they see the target because they assume that the player is already there. But the player covering the base may not be there yet, and the fielder cannot throw the ball until he sees the player in that spot. You are working on multiple fundamentals skills at one time.

Equipment

Baseball colored in half for each group playing catch

Number of Players

Full team

Setup

Line up team with the same number players on each side, as they would line up when playing catch. Players start with the head and eyes in the glove where the baseball is because that is where they would be when they follow the ball into the glove. Players receiving the ball are in a receiving position, and the players throwing the ball begin with the glove in front and the ball in the glove in a fielding position.

Procedure

1. On your whistle, the players with the ball begin to move forward with the back leg (the right leg for right-handed throwers and the left for left-handers).
2. As they move forward, they work on transferring the ball from the glove to the hand. They then throw while at the same time picking up the target.
3. As they move forward, they begin to come down in a circular motion with the elbows rising to shoulder level. They do all this in one smooth motion with rhythm.

Coaching Points

- When you yell, "Ready," the players get in their fielding position so that you can see that everyone is in the correct position before you blow the whistle.
- The players throwing the ball make sure that they are turned completely sideways and are moving forward to the target. This mistake is common because players think that they are completely turned when they are not. They have to feel the exact position and feel their bodies going forward. They can then use the whole body and momentum to throw the baseball with authority.
- Look for the players throwing the baseball to move forward, turn, and throw. The upper body should rotate like a Ferris wheel, not a merry-go-round.
- As the players with the ball rotate to throw after the move forward, make sure that they do not rotate the upper body too early. The rotation should occur as late as possible, and the head and chest should go toward the glove.
- The receiver should transfer the baseball and get to the throwing position quickly.

19. Hat

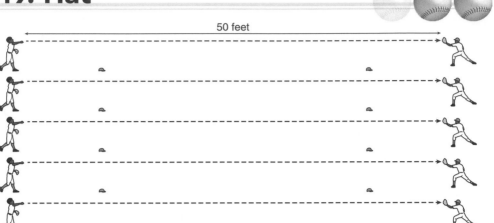

50 feet

Purpose

I received this drill from my good friend Tom House. This drill is done with the players farther apart. The players throw the ball straight and hit the ground. The receiver then fields the ball as a ground ball. One hoppers, two hoppers, and ground balls of all kinds are created by this drill. The idea is to place a baseball cap 10 to 20 feet in front of each player. The players then try to hit the hat with a throw. If they hit the hat, they are in line with the throw, the body is staying in line, and they are using the whole body, or at least most of it, to throw the baseball.

Equipment

Baseball colored in half for each group playing catch
Baseball cap for each player

Number of Players

Full team

Setup

Line up the players with partners. Move them back so that when they throw the ball as hard as possible, they are able to get it to their partners on the line. The players throwing the baseball can set up anyway they like, or you can dictate it according to what the players need to work on—starting sideways, fielding position, and so on.

Procedure

1. The players receiving the throw, which turns into a ground ball, field the ground ball and get into a throwing position.
2. Players throw the baseball on your whistle.

Coaching Points

*   When you yell, "Ready," players should get into the position you want them to be in so that you can see that they are in the correct position before you blow the whistle to throw.
*   You should watch to see that players are not opening up too soon with the glove side or the step because doing so will cause them to throw to the side of the baseball cap.
*   Look for the players throwing the baseball to move forward, turn, and throw. The upper body should rotate like a Ferris wheel, not a merry-go-round.

20. Quick Hands Throw Challenge

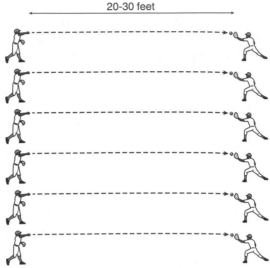

20-30 feet

Purpose

This drill is done last to get players to work on throwing the ball to each other at a close distance quickly but under control. It works the players' footwork, hand transfer, and ability to deal with pressure. The drill teaches players to throw the ball at short distances not hard but firmly. The ball should go straight, not with a hump.

Equipment

Baseball colored in half for each group playing catch

Number of Players

Full team

Setup

Line up the players with partners about 20 to 30 feet apart, depending on their age.

Procedure

1. Line up the players about 20 to 30 feet apart, depending on their age.
2. You whistle for players to start and then to stop. They see how many times they can throw the ball back and forth.
3. The players move farther apart when they are throwing the ball as hard as possible and are able to get it to their partner on the line.

Coaching Points

- Players should keep the hands out in front.
- Players should not make a long circle when throwing the ball because they want to throw it hard. They make a circle, but a short one, with the throwing arm.
- As the receiver catches the baseball, he begins to move his feet to get in a sideways position to throw the ball back.
- After the player throws, he retreats a step or two so that he can get into an athletic receiving position.

Variation

Use a stopwatch and time players for 30 seconds to see how many times they can get it back and forth to each other within that time.

21. Bad Grip Shuffle

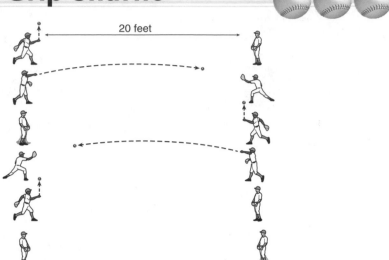

20 feet

Purpose

What happens if a player does everything well but does not have a good grip? Or what happens when the target player is not looking or not ready? What should the player do? The answer is that the player should shuffle the feet, keep or get the proper grip, and then throw the ball with rhythm. For example, when a ball is hit right back to the pitcher, he usually has plenty of time to throw the ball to first, but the first baseman may not be at the base yet. The pitcher should shuffle his feet until the first baseman gets to the base and then throw the ball in rhythm.

Equipment

Baseballs

Number of Players

Full team

Setup

Line up team with the same number players on each side. Each has a partner. Players on one side have baseballs.

Procedure

1. On your whistle, the players toss the ball up to themselves.
2. As soon as they catch the baseball, they throw it to their partner. This drill works on the entire process of catching, transferring, turning the body in a good position, and throwing.
3. When you blow the whistle, the partners throw the ball back.
4. After each line does it once, the players catch the baseball and shuffle one or two times before throwing. Then the players in the other line do the same.

Coaching Points

- Players must not throw the ball until their partner is looking. They shuffle their feet until he is ready.
- As they shuffle, they gain momentum. When they throw the ball, they keep their rhythm.
- They shuffle their feet because if their feet are moving as they throw the ball, the body will be in rhythm with the arms.
- Make sure that the players look before they throw.

Variation

After the players improve, you can yell for them to shuffle or throw as they are catching the baseball. If you yell, "Shuffle," they have to catch the ball, shuffle a couple of times, and then throw. If you yell, "Throw," they catch it, turn, and throw.

4

Fielding Drills

Fielding a baseball consistently is a difficult and specific fundamental skill for many reasons. The biggest reason is the fear that the ball will take a bad hop and hit you. That fear is real. Another reason, especially at young levels, is that players must get into an uncomfortable position to field the ball correctly and have enough time to throw out the runner. Players often lack the strength and flexibility that they need to get into fielding position. Once a player can take the proper fielding position without thinking about it, he has to learn to read the direction of the baseball, its velocity, and the timing of the hops so that he can get the ball when it is in the air and not when it hits the ground.

In the drills in this chapter, players work on tracking the ball all the way into the glove. This is a good habit to get into, along with getting low to the ground so that they can see the baseball better.

Types of Hops

Several kinds of hops can occur. First is the one hopper. The ball bounces up high on a big hop so that it is easy to catch. Many call it the Sunday hop, as if the Almighty is doing them a favor. Another hop is the in-between hop. The ball hits the ground maybe one to three feet in front of the fielder so it is at the midpoint of its upward bounce. The player has little time to react. Last is the hop that stays in the air longer. You want players to go after that one right away. You prefer that they get this ball on its way down because the ball on the way up can handcuff the fielder if he misjudges the speed of the ball. When the ball is in the air, it will not take a bad hop unless it is hit by a gust of wind, like a hurricane. So the ball in the air coming down is the one that you want players to read and go get it before it hits the ground again. Players should understand that the fewer hops a ball takes, the less likely it is that the ball will take a bad hop. At the same time they try to get in a situation where they can get the ball in the air coming down before it touches the ground.

Ready Position

Many people describe the proper fielding position as an athletic position like that taken in basketball, football, or other sports to guard someone. I like to describe it as an athletic position from which you could push off and run in any direction without coming down or up with your body. If you have to move up or down before pushing off and running, you lose time. Baseball is often called a game of inches, and time is one thing that you cannot afford to lose.

The athletic position normally has the player standing with the feet shoulder-width apart. The right foot is slightly behind the left foot for right-handers (opposite for left-handed throwers). The weight should be on the balls of the feet.

A way to demonstrate this to your players is to put them in the incorrect position by having them place their feet even, bend their knees slightly, and place the weight on their heels. If they lift their toes off the ground and start tapping the toes, the weight will be on the heels. Then have the players stagger their feet slightly and tap their heels. The weight is then on the balls of the feet (or the front part of the foot). When they feel the difference, they will understand the ready position.

In the ready position, the hands should be at the sides. If the ball is hit to the side, the first movement should be a push and turn to get the baseball. The head should be up, and by using their peripheral vision, players can see the pitcher and home plate. With this type of vision, players are able to track the baseball from release to the hitting zone without moving the head.

From this ready position, it becomes a challenge in understanding how to approach the baseball. This calculated movement can be quick, slow, or smooth or a combination of all three. The player's movement is determined by the velocity and direction of the baseball. It will also be determined by the infield position that the player is playing, the speed of the runner, and more. How the player goes forward in approaching the baseball is important. The player should take short, choppy steps starting with the right foot (if a right-handed thrower). As the player goes right, he goes with the left foot and keeps repeating right and then left toward the ball until he has to determine when he will be getting into the fielding position. Slightly early is always better than late because then the player will be fielding the ball between the feet, not out in front of the body. When the player begins to go into his fielding position, the key point is take a step out with the left foot on a slight angle so that the base is wider than the shoulders. The player can then lower the body a lot easier than he could if his feet were shoulder-width apart. As a coach, try both ways to demonstrate to yourself that you can more easily get lower with your feet wider than your shoulders. The other key is to bend the knees, not the back, so that the hands can get out in front of the body as far as possible.

An exercise that can help your players feel the difference between the good and the bad fielding position is to have them all stand with their feet wider than their shoulders and their hands out in front. Have them bend the back. They will feel the head and glove go between their legs. Have them start the same way but bend the knees, not the back. They will not only see the glove go out in front but also feel better.

Anticipating the Play

As players gain experience they need to work hard on several things. One is reading the pitch and the location—inside, outside, or middle of the plate. Knowing the location of the pitch will help them anticipate where the batter will hit the ball and allow them to get an early body lean or movement toward that area. They also need to understand the type of pitch—fastball, curve, or change—because the kind of pitch will cause the hitter to reach differently and hit the ball in a particular area. Finally, the bat angle of the hitter—whether the bat is behind the ball or in front at contact—will determine the area where the ball will be hit. For example, if the ball is deeper in the hitting zone, it will most likely be hit to the right side when a right-handed hitter is hitting. You can work on this in batting practice when you have only your regular position players on the field and no more (with young players you only want three outfielders because the infielders will begin to get bored). As the players take batting practice, the defense works on reading the hitter's bat angle and the velocity and type of pitch. Players can try to anticipate where the ball is going to be hit. Even if they are wrong, they learn a lot from the experience.

The following sequence of fielding drills can be done in various orders after players understand and can do them.

When beginning fielding drills and you're going to throw, start players close together to teach them proper technique. Then, as they get better at the technique, they can move farther apart to simulate game throws.

22. Fielding Position

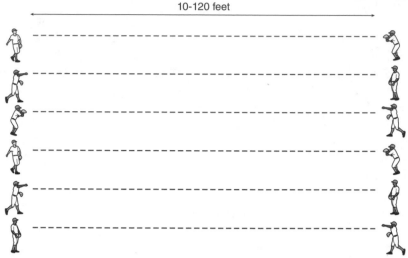

10-120 feet

Purpose

This drill helps players understand the fielding position so that when they get into the wrong position they will feel it immediately. In addition, players learn the position by doing it repeatedly and they will enjoy what they are doing, thus facilitating the learning process. Because they do this drill in every practice, they develop strength and flexibility in the muscles that allow them to get into that position. They learn how to go from the fielding position to the throwing position as they will be required to do in a real game.

Equipment

One baseball for every two players

Number of Players

12

Setup

Line up two groups of six players with partners facing each other. Have them 30 or 40 feet apart in the beginning. One group of players has a baseball in the glove, and the other group is in a ready position to catch the baseball. The players with the ball get into a fielding position on your whistle.

Procedure

1. When you whistle again, the players pretend to field the ball and throw it to their partner.
2. The partners catch the baseball and immediately go into the throwing position, working on receiving, transferring the baseball, and getting into a good throwing position.
3. When you whistle again, the players who have the baseball get into their proper fielding position.
4. This process continues for about 10 throws each.

Coaching Points

*   Look for the players in the fielding position to bring the glove up slightly and to the middle of the body as they begin to go forward and throw the baseball.
*   Check that all the players are in a good fielding position by having the fingertips of their gloves on the ground and the ball in the glove. The back of the glove should not be on the ground because this will cause the fingers of the glove to be facing up toward the sky.
*   Make sure that players are not touching the glove with the bare hand, which should be either to the side of the glove, on top, or even somewhere in the middle.
*   As they go through the proper fielding position, the back foot should be coming forward and the body should be getting into a throwing position by turning sideways.

23. Backhand Position

30-40 feet

Purpose

With this drill the players are in several backhand positions that simulate game positions. They have the ball in the glove and from that position throw the ball to their partner.

Equipment

One baseball for every two players

Number of Players

12

Setup

Line up players in two groups of six with partners facing each other. Do not have them too far apart to start, maybe 30 to 40 feet. Players in one group have a baseball in their gloves, and players in the other group are in a ready position to catch the baseball. The group with the ball gets into a backhand position when you whistle. This position, for right handers, has the right foot in a stride position to their right on a slight angle and the left knee on the ground. From this position, they come up slightly and push off the right leg to throw the ball to their partner. The glove should be slightly in front of the body so that the right knee does not block the glove hand from giving slightly to catch the ball.

Procedure

1. When you whistle again, the players all get into the backhand position with the right foot forward. They then give slightly with the glove, simulating the ball going into the glove. At the same time they keep the glove low to the ground and do not bring it straight up. From this backhand position, they move forward and throw the ball to their partner.
2. The partner catches the baseball and immediately goes into the throwing position, working on receiving, transferring the baseball, and getting into a good throwing position.
3. You then whistle again, and the players who have the baseball get into the proper backhand position.
4. This process continues for about 10 throws each.

Coaching Points

*   Make sure that the players' back knee is low to the ground and not straight up because this position causes the body to lean forward too much and be off balance. It also causes the head to be over the ball and not behind it, where they can see it better.
*   The glove should be out in front of the foot so that players have some room to give a little as they field the ball.
*   Players should give slightly with the fingertips of the glove low to the ground to absorb the shock. Most players come straight up with the glove, so the ball ends up going underneath it.
*   Players should take the first right or left step at a slight angle to gain some ground. This step helps put the glove at a better angle to receive the baseball.

Variations

In this variation, players use a backhand position but they start with the left foot forward. Then, as they pretend to field the ball, they take a step with the right foot and plant it, keeping the body low to throw the ball. In a real game, players can field the ball off the right foot or the left, depending on which one comes up. In a game they do not want to think. Instead, they just go into the position that their speed takes them and throw the baseball. They do not want to think about fielding the backhand off the right foot or the left foot. Whichever one comes up, they do it with that foot. Another variation of the backhand occurs when the ball is not hit hard and the player has to hurry to get to it. The player cannot get in front of it, so he gets to the side of it. As he is on the side of the ball, he shuffles his feet as he bends both knees to get down, field it off the backhand, and continue forward to throw the ball. He does this all in one motion. The glove is going low to the ground, and he fields the ball coming forward. He may have to come up slightly if the ball bounces up. To practice this, he starts turned sideways with the feet even with the ball in the glove and the glove on the ground. The player has to bend both knees, and then he shuffles a couple times to throw the baseball.

24. Forehand Position

30 feet

Purpose

With this drill the players are in a forehand position. Right-handed throwers turn to their left, and lefties turn to the right. They have the ball in the glove, and from that position they throw it to their partner. From the forehand position, they bring the glove from the ground to the middle of the body. At the same time, with the back foot they try to step inside toward the target, not behind the other foot because doing so will cause their momentum to fall away from the target. Players want their whole momentum going toward the target to get maximum velocity on the baseball.

Equipment

One baseball for every two players

Number of Players

12

Setup

Line up six players in two groups. Do not have them too far apart, maybe 30 to 40 feet, to begin. One group of players has a baseball in the glove, and the other is in ready position to catch the baseball.

Procedure

1. The group with the ball gets into a forehand position on your whistle. This position is with the left foot stepping to the left and the right knee on the ground. The glove should be out in front of the body, not behind it, so that there is some give when they field the ball. From this position, players bring the glove to the center of the body and step with the right foot toward the target. Both feet should move fast to get into a good position to throw the baseball.

2. When you whistle again, the players pretend to field the ball on the forehand position by giving slightly with the glove, keeping it low to the ground, and not bringing it straight up. Then they throw the ball to their partner.

3. The partner catches the baseball and immediately goes into the throwing position, working on receiving, transferring the baseball, and getting into a good throwing position.

4. When you whistle again, the players who have the baseball get into their proper forehand position.

5. This process continues for about 10 throws each.

Coaching Points

- Look for players to have the head over the center of gravity, which is their belly button when they are in the forehand position.
- The back knee needs to be low to the ground.
- Look for the glove to be out in front and near the ground so that if the ball takes a bad hop, the glove can come up and get it.
- The eyes should be on the ball all the way into the glove.
- Players should bring the glove to center of the body as they quickly move their feet to get into a good throwing position with the front shoulder pointed to the target.
- In the beginning, you want players to throw over the top to three-quarters so that the ball travels straight. They should aim to the outfield side of first base. If the receiver is a right-handed thrower, the fielder should throw to his throwing-arm side because the ball will tend to tail away from the receiver if it is thrown throw right at him.

Variation

Players are in a forehand position. A partner rolls the ball to the player's glove from a very close location. The player fields it, comes up, and throws the ball. This process can go back and forth by the partners. This drill takes the players from starting with the ball in the glove to having to field a ball rolling to the glove.

25. Roll in Front, Field, and Throw

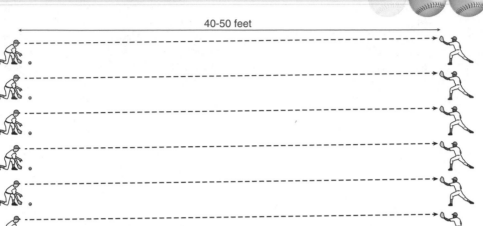

40-50 feet

Purpose

This drill works on a ball that gets past the fielder or a ball that deflects out in front. As the player gets into a fielding position, the ball may take a bad hop, hit him in the chest, and carom out in front. Players need to be taught that bad bounces and errors occur, but that what they do after that happens is what is important. They need to go get the ball with the proper technique so that they can quickly finish the play.

Equipment

One baseball for every two players

Number of Players

12

Setup

Line up two groups of six players. Do not have them too far apart in the beginning, maybe 40 to 50 feet apart. The players in one group each have a baseball in the glove, and their partners are in a ready position to catch the baseball.

Procedure

1. The players in the group with the ball get into a fielding position when you whistle. From this position, the players with the ball roll it out in front.

2. They then go to the side of the ball, fielding it, and throwing it to their partner. If the ball is rolling, they scoop it up with the glove and bare hand. If the ball has stopped, they come on top of the ball with the bare hand, jam the ball into the ground to get a good grip, and throw the ball to their partner. When reaching down with the bare hand, they bring the glove down as well to ensure that both shoulders and the head come down so that the focus is on the baseball.

3. The partner catches the baseball and immediately works on receiving, transferring, and getting into a good throwing position.

4. When you whistle again, the players who have the baseball get into their fielding position.

5. This process continues for about 10 throws for each player.

Coaching Points

- Make sure that players get to the side of the baseball, not behind it.

- If the ball is rolling, watch that players are scooping the ball with both the glove and the bare hand.

- If the ball is stopped, players should get it with the bare hand straight on top and push it into the ground.

- Players should always reach down with both hands when using any of the techniques.

- Players should never pick up the ball with the glove only because transferring the ball from the glove to the bare hand takes too much time and could lead to dropping the baseball during the transfer.

26. Roll Ball Behind

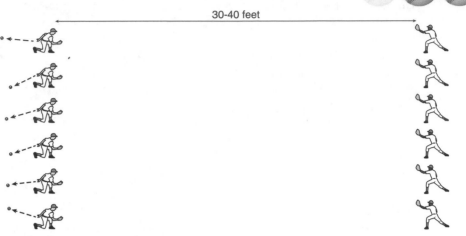

30-40 feet

Purpose

This drill works on a ball that bounds unpredictably and gets behind the player or to the side. As the player gets into a fielding position, the ball takes a bad hop and caroms behind him. Players need to be taught that bad bounces and errors occur but that what they do next is what is important. Do they continue to finish the play, or do they stop, put their heads down, and look beaten? Coaches need to train players how to react in real situations. What to do when errors or bad hops occur needs to become second nature. So here players start in the fielding position and then roll the ball behind them. From the fielding position they run hard (go slow when they do it the first time to get the body and mind used to it) and get to the side of the ball. The ball will be in the middle of the body. If the ball is rolling, the player scoops it up with both hands, takes a shuffle, and throws it. If the ball is not rolling, he reaches down with both hands so that the shoulders come down and the head and eyes go with them. Some players tend to reach with one hand, so the other shoulder and the head are up. They are thus looking for the base or runner and do not get the ball. The player reaches down with both hands, grabs the ball on top and pushes into the ground to make sure that he has it, and then goes forward with a shuffle and throws the baseball. Players should always have the head and eyes go down where the baseball is to field it.

Equipment

One baseball for every two players

Number of Players

12

Setup

Line up two groups of six players. Do not have them too far apart when you start, maybe 30 to 40 feet apart. In this drill they will end up farther apart because they are rolling the ball behind them. Players in one group have baseballs in their gloves, and players in the other group are in a ready position to catch the baseball.

Procedure

1. The players with the ball get into a fielding position on your whistle. From this position, the players roll the ball behind them on your next whistle. They should roll it to their right and left to practice both sides. They go get it, get to the side of the ball, and throw it to their partner.

2. The partner catches the baseball and works on receiving, transferring the baseball, and getting into a good throwing position.

3. Then, on your whistle, the players who have the baseball get into their fielding position.

4. This process continues for about 10 throws by each player.

Coaching Points

- Make sure that players get to the side of the baseball.
- If the ball is rolling, watch that the players scoop the baseball with the glove and hand.
- If the ball is stopped, players should get it with the bare hand straight on top and push it into the ground.
- They should always reach down with both hands in all of the drills.
- Players should never pick up the ball with the glove only.
- Players practice rolling the ball to both sides because it can go either way in a game.

27. Four-Corner Team Ground Balls

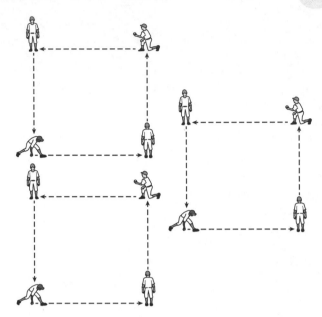

Purpose

This drill emphasizes work as a team on multiple ground balls. It allows you to observe and, if needed, pull a struggling player out of the group and work with that player as the group continues the drill. This drill can also be set up in three stations.

Equipment

Four or five baseballs

Number of Players

12

Setup

Set up three stations of four players about 50 feet apart and form a square. Place one player with no glove at each corner. Start with one baseball and go clockwise.

Procedure

1. On the whistle, the player rolls the ball to the person in the next corner, and so on.

2. With no glove, players have to bend their knees more to field the ball with two hands.

3. As they improve, go counterclockwise. Here they have to turn their feet fast and get into the position to roll the ball, which emphasizes quick feet.

4. As they improve, add a second ball at the opposite corner of the box, not two guys with a baseball next to each other.

5. Two baseballs give them more of a challenge and retains their attention. This is fun and competitive.

6. Once a ball gets by a player, blow the whistle and start again.

7. Challenge the players and ask them if they think they can do three baseballs. This is a lot of fun.

8. You are accomplishing lots of fielding in a fun, competitive way.

Coaching Points

- At first, make sure the players slow down to work on the fundamentals.
- Make sure they roll the ball straight at the player.
- Look for the fundamentals of bending the knees with hands out in front and positioning feet wider than the shoulders, along with one foot slightly behind the other for better balance.
- When they go counterclockwise, they have to move both feet by using a hip turn, which works on the lower-body turning.

Variation

They can put the gloves on and make the box bigger and roll the ball harder and bounce it. Eventually, if they improve enough, you can tell players they have to field the ball no matter where it is to the backhand position and the forehand. They can also field and drop and pick up and roll again.

28. Diving Position and Throw

60 feet

Purpose

This drill is specifically designed to teach young players how to dive for a ball on either side and come up quickly to throw the baseball. Kids love this drill because they love to dive and will love it more when they do it well. You will see players throwing the ball away in this drill because as they push up, they do not control their bodies to be in a flexed position. Instead, they come straight up, lean back, and throw it high. Teach them to control the head and core area. The core is normally weak, so the head, the heaviest part of the body, causes them to lean back, unbalancing the body. If they do not get in this position right away, you can ask the players to come up quickly but stop with their hands together by the chest area, turn sideways ready to throw, and check their body posture. Then you say, "Go," and they shuffle and throw. This pause in the sequence lets them feel the position that they need to be in before they throw the ball. In addition, teach them to pick up the target before they throw, which they worked on in the throwing drills.

Equipment

One baseball for every two players

Number of Players

12

Setup

Line up players in two groups of six about 60 feet apart. Each player in one group has a baseball in his glove, and the players in the other group are in a ready position to catch the baseball.

Procedure

1. On your whistle, the players in the group with the ball get into a diving position to their right, left, in front, or on an angle. You can even have them roll and get up and throw. On your next whistle, the players push up and throw the ball to their partners.

2. The partners catch the baseball and work on receiving, transferring the baseball, and getting into a good throwing position.

3. When you whistle again, the players who have the baseball get into their diving position lying down and the process continues.

4. This process continues for about 10 throws by each player.

Coaching Points

- Make sure that the players are lying stretched out on their bellies.
- Their hands and arms come close to their bodies to push up.
- They do not rise straight up.
- They pick up the target before throwing.
- After they come up, most players should shuffle and throw the ball to get momentum on the throw and put less stress on the arm, especially when they are making 10 throws in a row. You may want to keep the distance between the players short to reduce the stress on their arms. But they should practice both the dive with no shuffle before the throw and the dive and shuffle. If they have time they can shuffle; if they have no time they will not, depending on how fast the runner is and how hard the ball was hit.

Variation

After players do the diving drill, you want to start teaching them to dive into that position. As before, we are working backward into teaching the fundamental technique. They start on two knees and dive with the ball in the glove. As they hit the ground, they push up, come up, and throw the baseball to their partner.

29. Four-Corner Advanced Team Ground Balls

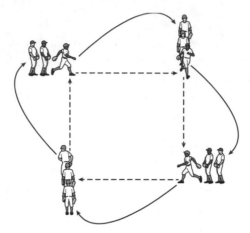

Purpose

You will make it more competitive so the players have to think more. Two players are at each corner. Incorporate rolling the ball and then following the ball. There is some conditioning, which will simulate the conditions late in the game when the body is tired and the mind needs to take over and stay focused on allowing the body to bend correctly.

Equipment

Four or five baseballs

Number of Players

12

Setup

Set up one station of three players in each corner of the box. Form a square about 70 by 70 feet. Players have gloves. Start with one baseball and go clockwise.

Procedure

1. On the whistle, the player will roll the ball to the guy in the next corner, and so on. After rolling the ball, the player will follow where he rolled it and go to the next group at the end of the line.
2. As they improve, go counterclockwise. Here they have to turn their feet fast and get into position to roll the ball, which works on quick feet.
3. As they improve more, add a second baseball at the opposite corner of the box, not two guys with a baseball next to each other.
4. Two baseballs give players more of a challenge and will retain their attention. This is fun and competitive and works on conditioning.
5. Once a ball gets by a player, blow the whistle and start again.
6. Challenge the players and ask them if they think they can do three baseballs. This is a lot of fun. We have done as many as four baseballs at one time.

Coaching Points

- At first, make sure the players slow down to work on the fundamentals.
- Make sure they roll the ball straight at the player.
- Look for the fundamentals of bending the knees with hands out in front and feet wider than the shoulders, along with one foot slightly behind the other for better balance.
- When they go counterclockwise, they have to move both feet by using a hip turn, which works on lower-body turning.
- As soon as a player rolls a baseball, he must hustle to the next line because another ball will be coming. They need to get out of the way; if they don't, it simulates a runner passing a ground ball as the fielder is trying to field it.

Variation

Make the box bigger so the players can roll the ball harder and bounce it. Eventually, if they get good, tell players they have to field the ball no matter where it is to the backhand position and the forehand. Also, add a field and drop and then pick up and roll again.

5

Hitting Drills

Hitting has been described as the single most difficult thing to do in sport. I agree that hitting is hard, but I wonder whether those who say that have ever downhill skied or raced a car at 200 miles per hour. It's also been said that hitting is hard because you have two round objects and you're trying to square them up. I'm not sure that two round items can be hit squared, but it's a pretty close analogy. Hitting is trying to place the big part of the bat behind the ball, so it's like hitting a wall, and the velocity of the pitch along with the velocity of the bat will do the rest. Hitting is also learning what to do when you get fooled by the pitch and not giving up. Or maybe it's giving up because it's only one strike and if you had continued to try to hit it with the swing, you would have made an out. Wow, that's a lot to think about when you hit, or is it?

Many have said that mechanics are important, but we have beaten this horse dead because kids everywhere work on their mechanics, and I do too, and we cannot hit. Why? Because the thing that has to be worked at the most is hard. Don't get me wrong; mechanics are important, but at the top of list are two things. First is being able to identify the pitch before or at release, along with the speed and location. All this needs to be done in about two-tenths of a second. The ball will be halfway to the batter by then, and the rest of the time is used to swing the bat. Second, a hitter also needs to be able to time a pitch with the help of recognizing the type of pitch first, velocity next, and then location. Within the two-tenths of a second, all the information needs to be calculated and used to time the pitch. So, to review, the important phases of hitting that players need to work at are mechanics (which is mostly the ability to maintain balance from start to finish and adjust to pitches with the hands), timing, and identification of pitches.

The drills that you are about to see have been designed in a sequence for some of the most important aspects of hitting. They work from the end part of the swing back to the original part, which is the stance. Many of us teach players beginning with the stance and then the action of going forward to hit the baseball. Here we teach it in reverse so that the players understand and feel the most important phase of the swing, the contact point, and the finish, which completes the swing and works on balance. The drills were designed for coaches who do not have a lot of time for practices, do not have much equipment, and need to work with a group of 12 to 14 players at a time. Players should be able to get their own feel about how the drill works so that they can continue to do it on their own.

30. Swing Warm-Up

Purpose

In this drill, players spend about five minutes working on their swing, starting at a slow speed and working up to game speed when they get comfortable. It works through the mechanics of the swing from the finish to the start and from the start to the finish. The drill warms up the players and works on their balance to get them ready for all the hitting drills they will do in practice.

Equipment

Bat for each player

Number of Players

12 or more

Setup

Place players in a big circle so that they can warm up swinging the bat. Players start with their arms straight out in front of them, pointing the bat straight up in the air.

Procedure

1. With their wrists, they drop the bat left and right parallel to the ground. They do this 10 times.

2. From the same position with the bat in front of them, they take the hands and bat, bring them over the head behind them, and feel the stretch. They then bring them in front so that the bat almost touches the ground. They do this back and front 10 times as the body stretches out.

3. The hitters start from the finish position of the swing. From this position they go backward to the contact point and back to the stance, and then from the stance to contact to the finish. They do this about 10 times to get the body loose.

4. The hitters begin in the contact position, the position where the ball and bat meet. From this position they come up to the stance, and as soon as the hands get back to the stance they take a full swing. They do this 10 times.

5. Finally, they get into the hitting stance and take 5 to 10 swings slowly to slightly faster, keeping their balance the whole time. Finally, they take 10 quick game-speed swings, keeping their balance the whole time.

Coaching Points

- Make sure that players start slowly and understand the swing.
- Eventually they do these drills at full game speed.
- They should challenge themselves to keep their balance on all the swings.

31. Contact Back to Contact Tee

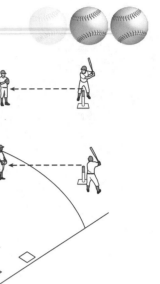

Purpose

This drill is used with a tee to help players understand the various contact points. This drill comes before drills in which someone tosses a baseball to the hitter. This approach is beneficial because the players have been to that spot and know how to get there correctly. Also, as they come back, their momentum will work on the weight movement on its own, so coaches do not need to discuss it.

Equipment

Four batting tees
20 Wiffle balls or softer baseballs

Number of Players

12

Setup

Line up four batting tees with a hitter and two fielders in front of each. Keep the distance from the batter to the fielders to at least the distance from which they are used to pitching and no closer. When you say, "Ready," the hitters get to the contact point with the bat and the fielders get in a ready position. Each hitter hits five to eight baseballs maximum before rotating.

Procedure

1. From the contact position, they bring the bat back up to the stance position. After the hands get back up to the stance, they make contact with the ball, taking the swing through the ball but not rolling the wrists over. It's not a full swing, but a half swing with a little bit of a follow-through.

2. The fielders try to field the baseballs on a bounce or a line drive.

3. The hitters try to hit as many line drives as they can.

4. After they hit all the baseballs, they rotate and someone else hits.

Coaching Points

- Look for the hitters not to roll their wrists before or after they hit the ball. They can follow through as far as they like without rolling their wrists.

- This is not a full swing; players only go back to contact and a little past the ball. It should not be done at full speed.

- When they start, make them swing slowly so that the body understands what it is trying to do.

- Fielders should try to field the baseballs on a line drive.

- Players should measure their distance from the ball by placing the barrel of the bat by placing the barrel behind the baseball, which is on a batting tee. The body will be in the proper position at the contact point, as discussed in the hitting section.

32. Contact Back and Hit

Purpose
In this drill, players start at the contact point. As they come back to their stance and their hands reach the area where they are supposed to be, they do not stop the momentum but go into a full swing. Players have been to that spot and now know how to get there correctly.

Equipment
Four batting tees
20 Wiffle balls or softer baseballs

Number of Players
12

Setup
Line up four batting tees with a hitter and two fielders in front of each one. The distance depends on what type of baseballs you are using and the players' age. Keep in mind that players are now hitting the ball, so you may want to use Wiffle balls or tennis balls. You can move the fielders back more because the hitters are taking a full swing. Keep the distance of the batter from the fielders to at least the distance from which they are used to pitching and no closer. Each hitter hits five to eight baseballs maximum before rotating.

Procedure
1. When you say, "Ready," the hitters and fielders get ready. When you blow the whistle, the hitters come back with the bat and hit the ball at contact with a full swing.
2. The fielders try to get the baseballs on a bounce or a line drive. They call for the baseball and work on communications.
3. The hitters try to hit as many line drives as they can.
4. After they hit all the baseballs, they rotate and someone else hits.

Coaching Points

- Look for the hitters not to roll their wrists before or after they hit the ball until they are in their follow-through.
- Fielders should try to field the baseballs on a line drive.
- As the players come back, their momentum and weight movement work on their own, so the coaches do not need to discuss it.
- After the players hit the ball and end up in their finish, they should freeze for a count of one-one-hundred.

Variation

Make the drill competitive by awarding points to the hitter for line drives and to the fielders for catching a ball in the air or fielding it cleanly.

33. Swing, Hit or Miss, Freeze

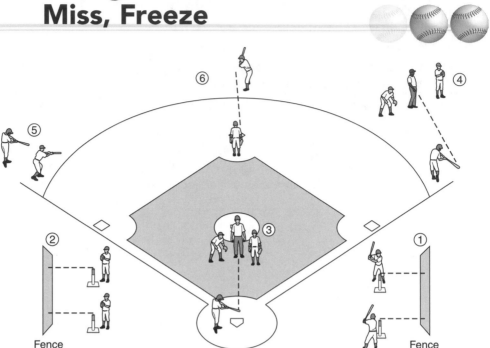

Fence   Fence

Purpose
This drill is especially designed for coaches who have little time to practice and to work on correcting the mechanics of the swing. Players get a good start and base from which to continue to work on other areas of the swing. The drill also teaches players how to hang on to the bat and drop it instead of throwing it. You cannot just tell a kid not to throw the bat or establish a penalty for throwing one; you have to teach them how not to throw the bat after the swing.

Equipment
Four batting tees

20 softer baseballs

20 Wiffle balls

Batting helmets

Number of Players
Full team

Setup
This drill should be done at the six hitting stations you have. The drill could be hitting off a batting tee, hitting a ball tossed underhand by a coach, hitting a ball thrown overhand by a coach on one knee, tossing the ball up and hitting it themselves, just swinging with no baseball, swinging during batting practice, any time.

Procedure

1. You have a coach who will yell ready, then whistle.
2. At the whistle, the drill begins and continues until players get 5-8 swings
3. Then you yell rotate and the players rotate to the next station.
4. This continues until everyone has completed each station.

Coaching Points

- Whether players hit or miss, they freeze the swing at the end and work on their balance.
- Remind players to freeze at the end. After a while it will become a habit.
- Tell players that as they work on this drill, they will miss the baseball more than they would like because they are mentally focusing on keeping their balance. This result is OK because as they improve their balance, they will switch their focus to the baseball.

34. Contact

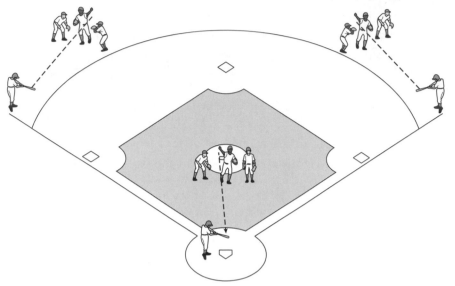

Purpose

This drill is similar to one I played when I was young called pepper, but at that time we often hit the ball on the ground by rolling our wrist early. This drill is important because it teaches young players the exact spot where the bat has to be when they make contact with the ball. When they miss the ball, it will show them why they missed it and where the bat was when they missed it. The idea is for the fielders to field the ball and throw it to the hitter. The hitter times it and stops the bat at contact with the baseball. Players learn to time the baseball and control the bat, so they are not always hitting the ball with a full swing during this drill. The drill also works on fielding and throwing the ball to a small strike zone area at a short distance. A lot of learning is going on.

Equipment

Three bats for three stations

Four players at each station

Extra baseballs in their back pockets or with the fielders

If possible, be by a fence for this drill because players will miss when first doing this

Number of Players

12

Setup

You begin with three fielders and one hitter about 20 to 30 feet apart. Depending on the players' age, this distance varies. Place hitters on the foul lines in the outfield and place the players on the outfield side. Use both foul lines and spread the players out so that not one gets hit by a ball coming from another group. Start with the players a little farther apart until they get used to it. Have the batter at least as far from the fielders as the distance from which they are used to pitching and no closer. The three fielders are about 5 feet apart. One player is throwing the ball to the hitter, and all three are ready to field a ground ball or line drive. The fielders should be about five feet from each other. Each hitter should take between five and eight pitches before rotating.

Procedure

1. The players fielding the baseball throw it to the hitter, and he hits it back.
2. The players throwing work on their throwing and fielding mechanics.
3. This drill can be done on your whistle. The players throw the ball, and you make sure that the hitter is in a good contact position before starting over.

Coaching Points

- Watch for the throwers to turn sideways before they throw the baseball.
- Watch for all the fielders to be ready all the time.
- Watch for the hitter to stop at contact. Have the hitters check their balance and key points—back heel up, the palm of one hand facing up and other down, front leg locked, and head over the back knee or belly button.
- Use soft baseballs when first doing this drill and build up to real baseballs if that is what players normally use. The two fielders without a baseball might have one in their back pocket in case the ball gets away too far or the hitter misses.
- If hitters roll the wrist over too early, they will either miss the baseball or, if they time it perfectly, pull the ball, usually foul.

Variations

Do this drill with three fielders when you start and then with two fielders. Then see how many players can do it one on one. You can also use this drill when a coach is throwing to a hitter. On the first 10 baseballs hitters stop at contact, and on the next 10 they can swing away. If a coach is throwing, there should be only a few fielders, not nine. Just put the outfielders out there and have them work on getting line drives, fly balls, and ground balls.

35. Timing

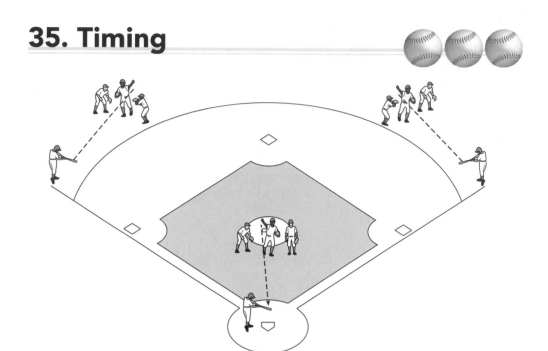

Purpose
This drill teaches players how to work on timing a baseball. Timing is a difficult skill to master, and the earlier that players begin to work on it, the better off they will be. We tend to wait until players have a great swing and can hit the fastball before we work on timing. But then players go into a game in which the pitcher has good control but throws the ball slow and slower. Players cannot hit it, and we wonder why. This drill is not easy at first, but as players do it for a while, they start to understand the concept and begin to learn what timing means. The ball occasionally lands short of the plate area, so the hitter has to take the pitch. The idea is for the hitter to see the ball coming out of the hand and judge whether it is slow or fast. If it is slow, then the hitter needs to come down slower with the front leg to time the ball and bat at the contact point. Players will see that if they start too soon, they will be off balance or will not be able to stop their momentum and will get to the contact point too early. The more often you do this drill, the more the players will understand timing without your having to teach anything.

Equipment
Three bats
20 Wiffle or tennis balls

Number of Players
12

Setup

Place one hitter on the foul line and three fielders in each group. You will have three groups of four players each. The fielders are in the outfield side of the field at about three-quarters of the pitching distance for that age group. Each player tossing the ball has five to eight balls.

Procedure

1. On your whistle, a player in each group tosses the ball underhand with a little bit of a hump on the toss.
2. The hitter goes to contact and tries to hit the ball back to the tosser.
3. After five to eight baseballs, the tosser switches with the hitter.
4. All the tosses are done on your whistle.

Coaching Points

- Watch how the players toss the ball.
- Watch hitters to make sure that they are not so anxious that they start their swing early. They can begin to go back and come back to center, but you do not want them turning to swing too early.
- As the hitters improve, the tossers can mix it up by tossing a ball in a straight line slowly, one with a hump, and another straight but faster.
- You are looking for the hitter to be on time with the front foot touching the ground.

36. Identifying Change, Curve, and Fastball

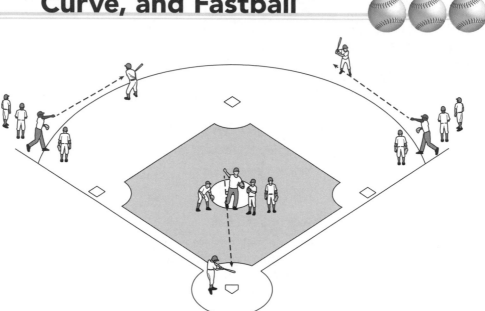

Purpose

Before doing this advanced drill, the players have worked on the timing drill and timing is becoming easier. This drill can also be used with advanced players who get bored because the drills are not competitive enough. This drill is a combination of tossing a baseball underhand and throwing three pitches—a fastball, a curveball, and a change-up.

Equipment

Baseballs

Bats

Number of Players

12

Setup

Place a coach with each group of four players. One player hits, and the other three field.

Procedure

1. The coach begins by tossing the ball underhand with a little hump, not on a straight line.
2. Hitters go to the contact point and hit the ball.
3. Fielders field the ball and give it to the coach.
4. Each hitter takes five to eight hits.
5. The next time around, the hitters get a straight underhand toss with no hump.
6. The next time around, as the coach releases the ball he turns his palm toward the ground. The ball will look like a fastball coming to the hitter, but because the coach turns his palm before release, the ball will slow down at the last moment.
7. The coach then spins the ball at release. This causes the ball to spin and not be straight; it looks and acts like a curveball.
8. The coach then determines when the players are ready for him to mix up the pitches so that they do not know what is coming.

Coaching Points

- Watch for players to time the ball and to get the front foot down right before they make contact. The players are not taking full swings but are stopping at contact.
- When the players do not know which pitch is coming, the situation will be more gamelike.

Variation

You can have a competitive game, and if a player gets a line drive, he continues to hit. If not, he is out and the next hitter hits. Players count how many times out of four or five at-bats they got a line drive.

37. Toss and Contact

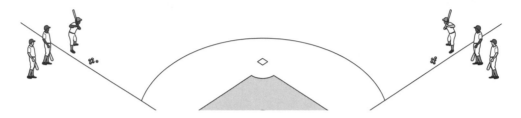

Purpose

Players can do this drill with fielders or alone. The hitter tosses the ball up and stops at contact. The goal is to hit as many line drives as possible out of 10 tosses. The hitter can hit into a fence or to one or two fielders out in front. He can toss the ball high in the air to simulate an off-speed pitch. He has to time the ball coming down and make contact. He can also toss the ball very short to simulate a fastball. He can toss the ball inside, middle, and away to simulate various contact points.

Equipment

30 baseballs
Two bats

Number of Players

12

Setup

Place one batter and one fielder on the foul line on the outfield side of the field. Each hitter has five baseballs.

Procedure

1. The player tosses the ball up, stops at contact, and hits the ball to a fielder.
2. He tries to hit as many line drives as possible out of five to eight tosses.
3. After five to eight tosses, the hitter switches with the fielder.

Coaching Points

- If the hitter tosses the ball poorly, he should take the pitch just as he would in a game.
- If he tosses the ball inside, he should pull it. If he tosses outside, he hits it away. If he tosses it middle, he hits it back up the middle.

Variations

You can place a fielder where the hitter will pull the ball, a fielder in the middle, and a fielder outside. The hitter tries to hit a line drive to each guy. He keeps going until he hits 10 baseballs. Also, the hitter takes the back foot and step over the front foot. As he steps, the front foot will come off the ground a little. The hitter will feel a load on the back leg and then toss and go to contact. This builds rhythm and teaches hitters how to load. So it's step, toss, and contact.

38. Tracking

Purpose

This drill helps players work on tracking a baseball from the pitcher's hand. They learn that the body might rotate but that the head moves slightly back to track the baseball. Also, when players hit off a batting tee, they should not look at the ball on the tee and swing but rather look out where a pitcher would be. Then, as they lift the leg and begin to hit, they turn the head to hit the ball to work on tracking.

Equipment

Four batting tees   Wiffle balls or soft baseballs

Four screens

Number of Players

12

Setup

Place a hitter on the foul line and a player acting as a pitcher on the outfield side. The player pitching should be at the distance used for pitching for the age of players you are working with. One fielder works with each pitcher to get the baseball. So you have four groups of three, each having a pitcher, a hitter, and a fielder. Each pitcher has five softer baseballs.

Procedure

1. You say, "Ready."
2. On your whistle, the pitchers pretend to throw the baseball.
3. Hitters watch the throwing hand of the pitcher as it comes forward and then direct the head and eyes at the ball on the batting tee. They hit the baseball off the tee.
4. The eyes and head move from the pitcher's hand at release to the ball on the tee.
5. If using a real baseball, the hitters hit the ball at contact and follow through, but they do not finish their swings.
6. If you are using Wiffle balls or very soft baseballs, the hitters can take a full swing off the batting tee.

Coaching Points

- Make sure that the hitters are watching the pitcher's hand as it comes to the point where the ball would be released.
- The head and eyes should then move from the pitcher to the ball on the batting tee.

Variations

This drill can be done in a cage with a coach or player pitching a baseball into a screen five feet in front of him and the hitter at home plate with a ball on the batting tee. The hitter watches the pitcher release the ball and then hits the ball off the batting tee.

The pitcher is behind the screen so that he is protected from the ball hit by the batter. In this case, the hitter takes a full swing.

6

Bunting
Drills

At many levels, bunting seems to be a lost art. I don't believe in giving up an out unless absolutely necessary. You have several other options that could produce the same result or better. Of course, anything you do must be practiced repeatedly. A coach should never ask a player to do something in a game that he has not practiced many times in a gamelike setting. In this chapter we review several bunting techniques. We outline the benefits of the style of bunting, and explain several ways to achieve the benefit of a sacrifice early in the game without giving up an out. We also review the fundamentals of the bunting position, which contributes to the ability to bunt the ball fair and in an area that is harder to defend.

With young players we have to keep a few things in mind. Their hands are not fully developed, so they have a hard time gripping the bat correctly. When they do not have a good firm grip, they are fearful of bunting, and most young players already have a fear of standing at home plate. The bunting stance could put them in an uncomfortable position that will increase their fear of standing at home plate.

Another aspect of bunting that young players have a hard time with is lowering the center of gravity to be more even with the ball coming to the plate. Instead of standing up and looking down at the ball, the player needs to get lower to see the ball better and get the plane of the bat on the same path as the ball. Achieving this position is important because it reduces the size of the strike zone.

Young players also have a difficult time keeping the bat even with the top of the strike zone. The main reason is the lack of strength on the backside, which raises the arms and elbows to allow it to stay there until the pitch arrives at home plate. An area that is overcoached is the catching of the baseball with the bat. When players give too much to catch the ball, the bat is too close to the body and not in a position to bunt the ball fair. The ball is past the eyes, so it is more difficult to see the ball when making contact with the bat. Giving too much with the hands to catch the baseball also causes many bunters to pop the ball up. The velocity of the ball and the natural reaction of the hitter to give a little with the bat is enough to deaden the ball. You do not have to mention to players to give with the ball. The bottom hand should be slightly up on the bat to permit more control. The palm of the hand should be on the bat, and that bottom hand controls the angle of the bat. A slight movement by the bottom hand creates the angle that the bunter is looking for to place the ball on the field where he wants it to go. The top hand should not be at the barrel of the bat but below it. The top and bottom hands should not be too far apart. This position is more stable and firm, which gives the player a sense of confidence that he has control of the bat. Being able to hold the bat with the right hand only (for a right-handed hitter) is a good test of whether the player has a good firm grip with the top hand. After the player has established this grip, have him grip the bat with the bottom hand. These two grips give the player total control of the bat and the confidence to bunt the ball fair.

The stance is as important as the areas just described because it is the foundation that puts the body in a positive position. If the foundation is off, then the rest of the body will be off and hard to control.

First is the traditional sacrifice bunt position that has been taught for years. The feet are shoulder-width apart, and the toes and the chest are facing the pitcher. The problem with this position is that it exposes the chest area of the hitter, which is dangerous, and it puts the hitter in a tough position from which to get out of the way of a bad pitch. It also puts the barrel of the bat farther from home plate. This position makes it hard to bunt a pitch down the middle or on the outside part of the plate.

The pivot bunt, in which the hitter pivots the back and front foot and gets into a bunting position, is widely taught, but it can be tough for young hitters because it puts them in an unbalanced position. In addition, bunting the middle to away pitch is difficult with the pivot bunt.

The sacrifice stance that I like most is the half-pivot stance because it's comfortable for players. This stance allows players to have a solid foundation, cover the whole plate, and have a better chance of protecting themselves from a bad pitch thrown at them. For the half-pivot stance, the player takes the back foot from the hitting stance and moves it forward slightly toward the plate. The front foot moves slightly back, which creates a half turn, instead of a full turn that has the feet and chest facing the pitcher. The half turn has the back foot facing home plate and the front foot facing the second-base position. This stance gives the bunter a solid base where he is in a good position to handle all pitches, including the tough outside pitch that normally forces a bunter to reach, fall off balance, and drop the barrel of the bat. On the outside pitch, just as with hitting, the player bunts the ball on the outside part of the plate, slightly back from the ball down the middle, most likely bunting it to the first-base side.

A sacrifice bunt is one in which the hitter gives himself up and puts down a bunt good enough that the defense has no choice but to throw the ball to first base. The key to the sacrifice bunt is to get in a bunting position as soon as the pitcher gets into a set position. Many bunters make the mistake of getting into the bunting position too late. They are off balance and create a bad bat angle, so a pop-up or bad bunt is the result. Bunters also make the mistake of moving toward first base to get a better jump as they are trying to bunt the ball. The result is often a pop-up because of a bad bat angle. The bunter needs to stay at home plate with the good stance that we described, good bat control, and the proper bat angle to bunt the ball in the right spot.

You can also call for a bunt, bunt for a hit, and steal play. This play is riskier than a bunt and no steal, but it can be tough on the defense. It does have the risk of a pop-up and being doubled off. When stealing, the runner should run hard but give a look at home plate so that he knows what is happening to the baseball. He can react faster on his own than by responding to a coach trying to get his attention and redirect him back to the base. In addition, if the runner looks to see what is happening with the baseball, he cannot be decoyed by the shortstop or second baseman, who may pretend that the ball has been popped up by calling for it when the ball has been hit on the ground. The runner who watches the decoying defenders may stop and go back.

Another option, the fake bunt and hit (runner not stealing), can be effective because when the defense comes in (this is too dangerous for players age 12 and under), the bunter pulls the bat back and hits. The goal here is to hit the ball hard on the ground so that it gets past the drawn-in or charging infield. On the fake bunt and hit, the hitter gets into a bunting position. As the pitcher begins to throw the ball, the hitter takes his top hand and slips it down with the other hand, which is slightly up on the bat. He draws the bat back to the hitting position and hits away. This play is like a hit and run, so you want to make sure that the hitter swings and tries to hit, unless it's a high pitch, in which case the hitter swings through it to protect the runner running.

You can also call for a fake bunt and steal. This play can be productive because the defense moves for the bunt and forgets to cover the steal. To execute it, the bunter makes it looks as if he is bunting. As the pitch comes in, he pulls the bat straight back so that the catcher has to wait a second before he comes forward.

I strongly believe in the sacrifice with two strikes. I believe that players focus more because they do not want to strike out. Your players need to know right away that they will be asked to sacrifice bunt with two strikes, so they need to be ready for it. More important, they need to practice bunting with two strikes against live pitchers.

The fake bunt delay steal is another good play to have in your repertoire of things to do so that you do not have to give up an out. You might see that the catcher is getting lazy and going to his knees or that the second baseman or shortstop is not backing up the pitcher on the throw back and covering the base. This situation is a good time to run a fake bunt and delay steal, especially if your runner is not superfast because he can catch the defense covering the bunt and not expecting the delay steal. The runner steals right as the catcher catches the baseball and is about to transfer the ball and throw it back to the pitcher.

Bunting for a Hit

The key to bunting for a hit is surprise and not trying to be moving to first as you bunt the baseball. Trying to run causes the bat to move and be in a bad position when bunting. The key to bunting for a hit is to wait until the pitcher is about to release the baseball and then get into bunting position. The pitcher then cannot change the pitch or the location of the pitch. The defense cannot adjust and get in early, especially the third baseman if he is playing back behind the base. If the bunter gets a good bunt down close to the third-base line, then it does not matter what the defense does because the bunter will have plenty of time to get to first base. Players should be encouraged to peek at the third baseman. If he is back, the hitter can put down a bunt on his own, not waiting for the coach to give him the sign.

Bunters who get out of the box early before they bunt are left-handed hitters because they normally use the crossover to bunt for a hit. With the crossover, the back foot of the left-handed hitter starts to cross over the right and head to first base. This action causes the upper body to move to first base too soon, and the upper body brings the arms, hands, and bat with it, preventing the bunter from covering the plate adequately. In addition, because of early movement toward first base, the barrel drops, often causing the ball to be popped up. Left-handed hitters can be successful by waiting until the pitch is about to be released before they get into a bunting position. A good technique here is for the bunter to wait until the pitcher is about to release the ball, take a short step toward the plate or pitcher with the left, or back, foot, put the ball down, and then run. He is in a much better position and balance to get a good bunt.

39. One-Knee Bunting

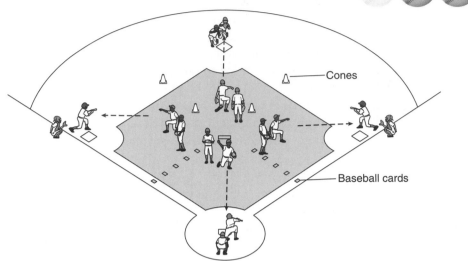

Cones

Baseball cards

Purpose

This drill isolates the upper body so that the player learns to use that part of the body first. If he can handle the bat well with his hands, then the rest becomes much easier.

Equipment

Four home plates or bases

20 baseballs

20 Wiffle balls or softer baseballs

20 baseball cards or 8 cones

Four bats

Number of Players

Full team

Setup

You have four stations with a home plate or bases, pitcher, a catcher, and a fielder by the pitcher. On a field, each base would be a home plate. The distance of the pitcher to the batter depends on the field that you are on. The person throwing the pitches will be on one knee. The bunter is on one knee—the right knee for a right-handed hitter and the left for a lefty. The bunter should have the knee and the front foot at the same angle that we described for the stance that we like. The front knee is slightly flexed. It's the same stance, and the player goes to one knee, the back knee. On the first- and third-base lines, lay down five baseball cards on each side. The bunter tries to bunt the ball to land on or roll over a card. If he is successful, he gets to keep the card. Alternatively, you can use two cones. If a player bunts through the two cones, he gets a baseball card as a reward. The reward makes them concentrate more. Just bunting can be boring.

Procedure

1. For the first round, you can have players hold the bat with the top hand only and try to bunt. Use Wiffle balls to reduce the fear factor and allow them to work on the fundamental skill.

2. For the next round, they use two hands and work on bunting down both lines. You can also play the game with the baseball cards.

Coaching Points

- Watch that the players have the correct grip on the bat. The hands control the bat, so the grip is crucial.

- Watch the bat angle. Is it parallel or on an angle?

- The barrel should be over and in front of the plate so that everything is bunted fair, not foul. In addition, having the hands out and keeping a slight bend at the elbows (not locking them) helps to deaden the ball.

- Look for the player to follow the ball all the way to the bat.

- At first, do not bring out the baseball cards when bunting. Have the players concentrate on the technique. Then, as they improve and become more confident, add the baseball cards to create more pressure. They receive a reward if they do well and nothing if they fail.

Variation

Instead of baseball cards, you can place two orange cones down the lines. The players try to bunt the ball between the cones.

40. Bunting Standing Up

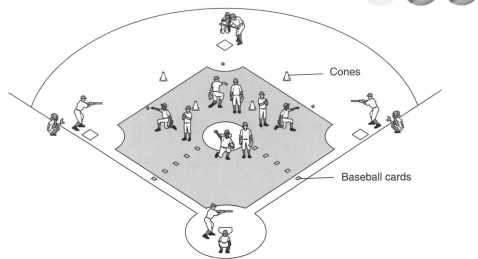

Cones

Baseball cards

Purpose

As the players become comfortable controlling the bat with their hands, you can start working on the lower-body stance. The best approach is to work backward, from the stance to the hitting position and then back to the stance. For this drill, you put them in the sacrifice bunt stance and bunt baseballs. Pitchers or coaches throw. For very young players, a coach throws from a knee. Then, as the players get a feel for how the lower and upper body work, they start in the hitting stance and go into the sacrifice bunting stance. Young players need to learn the sacrifice bunt before they start with the bunt for a hit.

Equipment

Four home plates or bases

20 baseballs

20 Wiffle balls or softer baseballs

20 baseball cards or 8 cones

Four bats

Number of Players

Full team

Setup

You have four stations with a home plate or a base, a pitcher, a catcher, and a fielder by the pitcher. If you use a field, each base would be a home plate. The distance from the pitcher to the batter depends on the field that you are on. The person throwing the pitches will be on one knee if the players are young and standing if they are older. Place the bunter in the stand-up sacrifice bunt position. On the first- and third-base lines, lay down five baseball cards on each side. The bunter tries to bunt the ball to land on or roll over a card. If he is successful, he gets to keep the card. Alternatively, you can use two cones. If a player bunts through the two cones, he gets a baseball card as a reward. The reward makes them concentrate more. Just bunting can be boring.

Procedure

1. For the first round, you can have the players hold the bat with the top hand only and try to bunt. Use Wiffle balls to reduce the fear factor and allow them to work on the fundamental skill.
2. For the next round, have then use two hands and work on bunting down both lines. You can also play the games with the baseball cards.

Coaching Points

- Watch that the players have the correct grip on the bat. The hands control the bat, so the grip is crucial.
- Make sure that they use the right lower-body stance because it gives them better balance, good plate coverage, and the confidence to bunt.
- Watch for the bat angle. Is it parallel or on an angle?
- The barrel should be over and in front of the plate so that everything is bunted fair, not foul. In addition, having the hands out and keeping a slight bend at the elbows (not locking them) helps to deaden the ball.
- Look for the player to follow the ball all the way to the bat.
- At first, do not bring the baseball cards out when bunting. Have the players concentrate on the technique. Then, as they improve and become more confident, add baseball cards to create more pressure. They receive a reward if they do well and nothing if they fail.

Variation

If your pitchers are ready, have the hitters practice the sacrifice bunt off live pitching. This variation puts your pitcher and catcher in a sacrifice situation. At some point, players will have to bunt off live pitching.

41. Four-Corner Bunting With a Variation

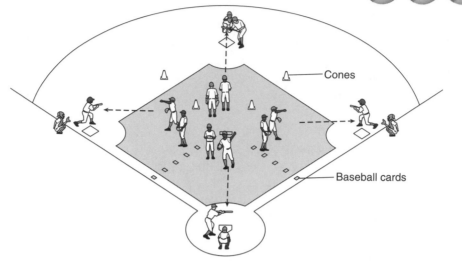

Cones

Baseball cards

Purpose

This drill works on bunting at all four bases as well as getting out of the box after bunting the ball. It also allows players to work on bunting for a hit.

Equipment

Four home plates or bases
20 baseballs
20 Wiffle balls or softer baseballs

20 baseball cards or 8 cones
Four bats

Number of Players

Full team

Setup

You have four stations with a home plate or a base, a pitcher, a catcher, and a fielder by the pitcher. If you use a field, each base would be a home plate. The distance from the pitcher to the hitter depends on the field that you are on. The person throwing the pitches will be on one knee if the players are young and standing if they are older. As you say, "Ready," the pitchers get into a stretch position, simulating a real game.

Procedure

1. The bunters get into a sacrifice bunt position. When you say, "Go," the pitchers pitch. The hitters bunt, and after they bunt they advance to the next base.

2. For the next round, when you say, "Ready," the pitchers go into the stretch. They can throw whenever they like. The bunters needs to get ready on their own, get the bunt down, and go on to the next base.

3. For the next round, it's the same situation but now a runner is at second. The bunters are bunting for a hit. At the other two bases they sacrifice.

4. For the next round, if the hitter bunted for a hit, he sacrifices and vice versa. You always say, "Ready."

Coaching Points

- Watch for the bunters to be getting ready at the right time.

- Watch that they do not get out of the box too early.

- As in a game, the bunters drop the bat and the next player uses the same bat. Players must learn to adjust with bats and learn how to control the bat.

- Watch how the bunters come out of the box. If they are balanced, they will come out much better. In addition, note where their first step is after they bunt. Is it back, toward the pitcher, or toward first base?

Variation

On the first- and third-base lines, lay down five baseball cards on each side. The bunter tries to bunt the ball to land on or roll over a card. If he is successful, he gets to keep the card. Alternatively, you can use two cones. If a player bunts through the two cones, he gets a baseball card as a reward.

42. Two-Corner Bunting

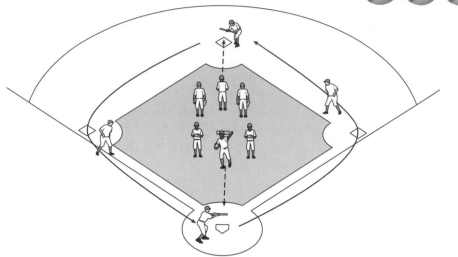

Purpose

This team drill incorporates some baserunning along with bunting. You can use several bunting situations with this drill, so use your imagination.

Equipment

Two bases   Two bats
20 Wiffle balls

Number of Players

Full team

Setup

Set up bunters at home and second base along with your pitchers, catchers, and fielders. You can also set up a runner on first and a runner on third. Pitchers are in their signal-taking position when you say, "Ready."

Procedure

1. You call out a situation and then say, "Go." The pitchers, at their own pace, throw the pitch, and the hitter and runner react. The runner takes his secondary lead. When he see the ball going to the ground, he heads for second base. When he gets to the next base, he gets in line to be a bunter.
2. You can have two bunters at each base and two runners at each base.
3. You can set up several situations—a bunt and steal, a fake bunt steal, a fake bunt hit.

Coaching Point

*   You are looking for all the things that you were looking for in the previous drills.

43. Bunting Game With Pitchers

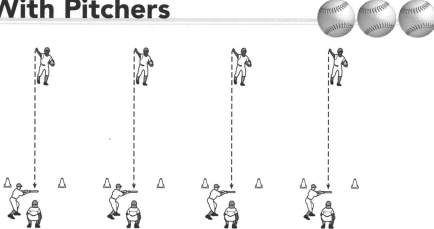

Purpose

Use this drill when you want to start getting your pitchers, catchers, and hitters ready to start bunting off live pitching. This can be done indoors or outdoors.

Equipment

Multiple sets of catcher's gear

Helmets

Bases

Baseballs

Cones

Number of Players

Full team

Setup

Line up as many pitchers as you have catchers. If you have only one catcher, set up a target by a fence and the pitcher can throw to that target. Have a bunter with a helmet on.

Procedure

1. Pitcher gets 12 to 15 pitches and then another pitcher replaces him.
2. Bunter decides when to bunt. If he decides to sacrifice, he will be bunting at strikes. If not, he will pull the bat back.
3. He can also decide to bunt for a hit or push the ball down the first-base side between the first baseman and pitcher.
4. Place two cones by both lines as a target.
5. You can make this into a game by seeing how many successful bunts the bunters have after 12 to 15 pitches.

Coaching Points

- Look for good bunting techniques.
- Keep a chart on good bunts.

44. Game Situation

Purpose

This drill puts the players, both the bunter and the defense, in a game situation. By allowing the play to finish under real game pressure, you can review the overall execution.

Equipment

Bases   Bats
Pitching mound   Baseballs
Helmets   Catcher's gear

Number of Players

Full team

Setup

Set up a full infield with a catcher in full gear. All hitters have helmets on at home plate and the bases. This is a real situation with a runner on first and no one out.

Procedure

1. The bunter has to sacrifice the runner over on any pitch he likes.
2. The defense can start in because they know that the hitter is trying to move the runner over.
3. You can use a point system. If the bunter gets a good bunt down but does not get the runner over, he still gets 1 point. If he gets the runner over, he gets 2 points. If he gets the runner over and is safe, he gets 3 points.
4. After three outs, you switch your defense to bunting and vice versa.
5. Depending on how well the bunters are doing, you can let the runners stay or start on first and second and try to get the runners over.
6. As they improve, you can add more to this game. Allow the hitters to swing or sacrifice bunt to keep the defense in a real game situation where they do not know what the hitter will be doing. If the hitter swings and hits a ball over the jumping defender, he is out. If the ball is not hit above the defender, it is considered a hit.
7. When you feel comfortable, you can add outfielders and finish all the plays, which will create different situations.

Variations

Add coaches to give signs. Allow the hitters to bunt for a hit, sacrifice bunt, fake bunt and hit, and fake bunt steal. The hitter decides what to do depending on where the runners are and how many outs there are. You can even have the players devise a sign system and have the hitter give a sign to the runners. This approach gets the players more involved in making decisions and giving signs.

45. Bunting Game
With Three Stations

Purpose
Multiple groups work on the sacrifice bunt and also defend it in a live situation. You can add a bunt for hit and steal or any of the bunt offenses already mentioned.

Equipment
Two sets of plastic bases   Bats
Baseballs   Helmets

Number of Players
Full team

Setup
Set up three fields with full infields. One team of players is on the field. The other two will use plastic bases in left and right field. You will have a full infield; if short of players, then skip having a third baseman or a runner on first.

Procedure
1. Pitchers throw, and bunters try to sacrifice the runner over and bunt the ball to the first-base side trying to bring the first baseman in.

Coaching Points
- Let the players make the play. Observe; if they do something incorrectly, stop and run through the play and let them know how you would like it.

- Pitchers will be throwing off flat ground. If they are not ready to throw fast, bring them in a few feet to increase the velocity.

7

Pitching Drills

Pitching is another specific fundamental skill that is physiologically hard for young players because of the size of baseball, the mechanics needed to throw the baseball consistently, the pressure when runners get on base, the pressure from the stands, and the players' lack of strength and overall coordination. As a coach of younger players, you should make it a priority to teach all your players to pitch, so you could have as many as 12 to 14 pitchers on your team. Their pitch counts will be limited because many players are pitching. You still want to place pitchers in positions to be successful. You also want to challenge pitchers when the competition level for them becomes too easy by pitching them against better hitters. Players need as much failure in their development as success because they need to recognize that the game will get tougher as they get older. They will learn that they need to work hard and smart all the time to be the best they can be at all levels. As a coach you need to recognize the right situation for each pitcher.

Ball Size

The baseball is too big for many young players. Even with great mechanics it is difficult for them to throw a baseball consistently over a 17-inch plate and in a 2-foot strike zone. Finally, it is difficult for young players to protect themselves when the ball is hit right up the middle. The Japanese have gone to using a smaller baseball for young players so that they are able to grip it correctly and not have issues with the mechanics. The normal baseball, 9 inches in circumference and 5 ounces in weight, is too heavy for young players and difficult for them to grip. They have the same problem that adults with small hands have when they try to throw a 12-inch softball or, even worse, the 16-inch softball that we play with in Chicago. An adult cannot throw a 12-inch softball with the same speed that he can a regular baseball. A heavy ball that the player cannot grip causes the elbow to drop because he must turn the hand over to hold the baseball. Even with great mechanics a young pitcher at release cannot grip a large ball properly, which results in an inconsistent throw. A proper grip allows the baseball to be released so it has a much better chance of traveling straight. And if the player can grip across the four seams of the baseball, the seams will grab the air particles from the top of the baseball and place them underneath as the ball travels, which allows a straighter and faster throw.

Pitching Mechanics

When players are young, you want the ball to go straight so that it stays consistently over the plate. One thing we do know is that young hitters have a hard time hitting any baseball over the plate, so the pitcher who can throw strikes consistently has a big advantage. Against better hitters, the pitcher needs to be able to start spotting the baseball in different locations. If a pitcher can place the ball at different locations, the hitter will not be as successful because his eyes have to keep changing positions and can never get used to one path of the ball. Keep in mind that pitchers are doing this at full speed, under pressure, and with a difficult time gripping the ball, so the ball is not always balanced at release. In addition, they need to keep the wrist straight at release so that the ball has a better chance of staying straight. For every inch that the wrist is bent to either side, the ball travels about 6 inches to that side. Home plate is 17 inches wide, so the margin for error is small.

For young players, the mechanics of pitching are almost identical to those for throwing a baseball. The simple difference is in the stride leg and knee. The knee lifts to about hip level for energy, timing, and synchronizing the body to have a linear movement toward home plate. Because the windup is much harder for young pitchers and they do not have time to work on it enough to control the body, they are better off pitching from the stretch position (described later). Starting from the stretch eliminates the need to wind up and then control the body to get into the balanced position before throwing. It's much easier to start from the stretch position, lift the leg, and fall toward home plate. The windup causes young players to throw the body off balance. Like hitters, pitchers need to start balanced, stay balanced as they are pitching, and finish balanced so that they are in a good position to protect themselves from a ball hit up the middle.

Balance

Balance is a key to all the fundamental skills, and you must emphasize this point to young players. Pitchers start from the stretch, lift the knee and leg, and get to the balance point. Without stopping at the balance point, they continue to go home by falling forward and directing the front shoulder, front elbow, and head home as long as possible. The longer they can keep the front side of the body going toward home before throwing the baseball, the later they will release the ball and the quicker the ball will get home. If they work on taking the front side home as long as possible, their control will improve. After they lift the leg, many young pitchers have a tendency to open up that leg like a gate before they go home. This action causes the whole body to start going in the wrong direction. If a pitcher does this, have him concentrate on the having the front shoulder going home as long as possible and not opening up the front leg. You can stand behind a player so that he feels when he is opening up too soon with the front leg.

The following drills are set up to begin warming up the players and getting their bodies to understand the correct movements of pitching a baseball. The sequence is simple to help the players get started and allow coaches to teach a group of pitchers. I highly recommend that all your players work on these drills because they improve their throwing mechanics. Players at a young age can do these drills because they also help increase flexibility, strength, and balance.

46. Speed and Accuracy

Purpose

This drill helps players establish control of the body in the off-season, reduces stress on the arm, and works on grips. Early in the year up until about a month before the season starts, players should work on their pitching on flat ground so that they put less pressure on their joints. They have no reason to be throwing off the mound in the winter. Also, keeping the distance close will not hurt their arms and will teach them how to control the speed of the ball. If you place them at regular distance right away, they throw the ball hard all the time and learn just one speed. If catchers are unavailable, make targets about the same size as the strike zone of an opposition player of average height. Start with a smaller home plate. A regular one is 17 inches. Start with a 13- or 14-inch plate. You can make them out of cardboard. Then, as your pitchers get good with a smaller plate, you advance them to the regular size. After they become proficient at locating the ball with a four-seam grip at the short distance, they can move back to the regular pitching distance for their age group. To some people, being proficient at location means throwing strikes, but to me it means being able to locate the ball 8 out of 10 times at the catcher's right and left knees and in the middle at his knees. Then pitchers need to locate it at the catcher's shoulders and mask. When they are good at that, they should be able to throw across—one away and one in at the knees and then the same at the shoulders. Finally, they work on crisscrossing from down and away to up and in for strikes, and then down and in and up and away.

Equipment

Baseballs
12 home plates (can be cut out of cardboard or colored paper plates)

Number of Players

12

Setup

Partners throw to each other at a distance of half their normal pitching distance. One is the pitcher, and the other is the catcher.

Procedure

1. When you say, "Signal," the pitchers look in for a sign. The players catching drop one finger for a four-seam fastball and give a target in the middle of the small plate.

2. When you say, "Stretch," all the pitchers go to the stretch.

3. When you say, "Pitch," the pitchers deliver a pitch that should be straight and firm but will be slow because of the short distance. In this case, pitchers are learning to control the speed and their bodies because they are closer than they are in a game.

4. After the catchers receive the baseball, they become pitchers and the pitchers become catchers.

Coaching Points

- Make sure that the players have a good four-seam grip so that the baseball rotates well and the ball goes straight.

- Watch to make sure that the pitchers are under control and are directing the head and eyes toward the target as they are delivering the baseball.

- Watch that the pitchers have good mechanics but are able to control the speed of the ball so that it is not fast but does go straight.

- Watch that the pitchers consistently hit the target down the middle, which will be the catcher's glove.

- Watch that the pitchers take the hand with the baseball to the target.

47. Four- and Two-Seam Grip to the Corners

Purpose

After establishing the four-seam grip down the middle, players need to establish it inside and outside of the plate. When players can do all this consistently with a four-seam grip, they are ready for the two-seam grip. The two-seam grip tends to move in various directions depending on the grip. If a pitcher can master all this, he has developed several pitches. Anyone who can master this at a young age can get many hitters out with just a fastball. Having good mechanics and working on the fastball gives the pitcher a consistent release point, which allows him to go to a second pitch more easily. By throwing at a shorter distance, pitchers also master what is called a batting-practice fastball, or BP fastball. This fastball is straight but is not thrown as hard. This pitch throws off the hitter's timing and starts the pitcher on the road to developing a changeup.

Equipment

12 baseballs

12 home plates (cut out of cardboard or colored paper to a smaller size, 12 to 14 inches instead of 17 inches)

Number of Players

12

Setup

Partners throw to each other at a distance of half of what they normally pitch from. One is the pitcher, and the other is the catcher.

Procedure

1. When you say, "Signal," the pitchers look in for a sign. The players catching drop one finger for a four-seam fastball and give a target to the outside part of the plate, as if a right-handed hitter is standing at the plate.

2. When you say, "Stretch," all the pitchers go to the stretch.

3. When you say, "Pitch," the pitchers deliver a pitch, which should be straight and firm but will be slow because of the distance. In this case, the pitchers are learning to control the speed and their bodies because they are closer than they are in a game.

4. After the players catching receive the baseball, they become pitchers and the pitchers become catchers.

5. After the pitchers have worked on 10 pitches to one side, they switch to throwing inside to a right-handed hitter.

Coaching Points

- Make sure that the players have a good four-seam grip so that the baseball rotates well and goes straight.

- Watch to make sure that the pitchers are under control and direct the head and eyes toward the target as they are delivering the baseball.

- Watch that the pitchers have good mechanics but are able to control the speed of the ball so that it is not fast but does go straight.

- Watch that the pitchers consistently hit the target on the outside corner, which will be the catcher's glove.

- Watch that the pitchers take the hand with the baseball to the target.

48. Slow-Motion Mechanics

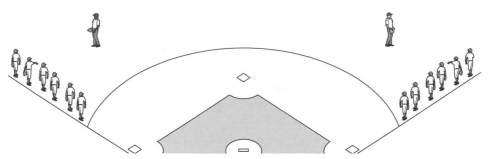

Purpose

This drill can be used for a warm-up as well as a way to teach the mechanics to young pitchers. The drill here starts someplace between the ready and fielding positions, which was described in earlier chapters. This position shows players where they should end up after throwing the baseball and give them a better chance of protecting themselves from a ball hit up the middle.

Equipment

Baseballs

Number of Players

Full team

Setup

Line up the players on a line. You could use a foul line of the field, which they could use as the rubber of the pitching mound. All the work is done on flat ground. Each player holds a baseball in his hand. To begin teaching this process, have all the players go from the stretch. After they know how to do it from the stretch, teaching the windup is much easier.

Procedure

1. On the first whistle, have the players go from the stretch to the balance position. On the second whistle, have them land and stop. On the third whistle, have them throw and finish in the follow-through position described earlier.

2. You now reverse the process from the follow-through and have them get to the landing position and then the balance position. They just jump back and get into the landing position.

3. Keep doing this process until the players get a good feeling of the positions they should be in throughout all phases of pitching.

Coaching Points

- In each phase make sure that they are balanced and that they feel comfortable. The players have to feel it when it is correct.
- Watch for how they control the head and upper body, which can take them into an off-balance position.
- Make sure that player safety comes first and that fielding the ball is secondary. From the fielding or ready position, a pitcher can field a grounder or catch a line drive.

Variations

Line up the pitchers as if they are going to play catch. They do the same drill, but in the landing position they now throw the ball to the partner and get into the position that allows them to get a ball hit right back at them. When they are ready, you have the partner roll or throw a baseball at them. Use softer baseballs at first and let your players know that they do not have to throw the ball hard. After catching the ball, the players reverse the process, going backward and getting all the way back to the balance position. As they get there, they get into the landing position and throw the baseball. As they throw, the body should bring them into the ready position to catch the ball.

This drill can be done from any of the positions. For example, the pitcher can be in the balance position and from there throw the baseball to the partner. The partner throws or rolls the ball back. First, make sure that they can do it from the landing position because they have to be in a perfect landing position to have a good chance to throw the ball over the plate. If they are not in a good landing position, they could be putting a lot of pressure on the joints, which could result in injuries.

49. Changeup

Purpose

After pitchers have developed good control of the fastballs described earlier, they are ready for the changeup. For young pitchers, the changeup requires only a different grip, which makes the ball go slower. Pitchers should not alter anything except the grip. They throw it just like the fastball so that they can focus on location only. They can use several grips and experiment to find the one that results in the slowest pitch. They can also use different grips for the changeup so that they have different speeds. Remember that pitching is about disrupting the hitter's timing. Pitchers who can do this will be successful. For one changeup grip, the pitcher grabs the ball with the whole hand and puts it deep into the palm. Keep in mind that because many young players can grip a regular-size baseball only by using the whole hand, they are always throwing a changeup. Another grip uses the whole hand and lifts the fingertips off the baseball, relieving the pressure points. They can also grip the ball with three fingers spread and the thumb and pinky underneath the baseball. Finally, they can use the same grip and lift the fingertips off the baseball, which relieves pressure on the ball. These grips are just some of the basic and easy one that young pitchers can work on, depending on their hand size and finger length. The ball will react differently for everyone.

Equipment

12 baseballs

12 home plates (cut out of cardboard or colored paper to a smaller size, 12 to 14 inches instead of 17 inches)

Number of Players

12

Setup

Partners throw to each other at a distance of half of what they normally pitch from. One is the pitcher, and the other is the catcher.

Procedure

1. When you say, "Signal," the pitchers look in for a sign. The players catching drop two fingers for a changeup and give a target to the middle part of the plate.
2. When you say, "Stretch," all the pitchers go to the stretch.
3. When you say, "Pitch," the pitchers deliver a pitch, which should be straight and firm but will be slow because of the distance. In this case, the pitchers are learning to control the speed and their bodies because they are closer than they are in a game.
4. After the players catching receive the baseball, they become pitchers and the pitchers become catchers.

Coaching Points

*   Make sure that the pitchers have a good changeup grip so that the baseball rotates well and the ball goes straight.
*   Watch to make sure that the pitchers are under control and direct the head and eyes toward the target as they are delivering the baseball.
*   Watch that the pitchers have good mechanics but are able to control the speed of the ball so that it is not fast but does go straight.
*   Watch that the pitchers consistently hit the target down the middle, which will be the catcher's glove.
*   Watch that the pitchers take the hand with the baseball to the target.
*   Watch that the pitchers are not changing anything from the motion that they use to throw a fastball.
*   Pitchers should start to feel how the grip works at release and get a good feel for how it comes out of the hand. The pitch should look like a fastball.

50. 21 Outs

Purpose

Selling your young players on working only on fastballs is not easy. Players see their friends throwing three or four pitches. Many of them cannot throw strikes, but they look cool doing it, so your players want to do the same thing. One of the best coaches I have ever been around, Dick Birmingham from Springfield, Missouri, showed me a game that you can play with your pitchers to show them that they can get hitters out on just fastballs. He used 21 outs, but you can use as many outs as you like. I like to use just 3 outs for young players and switch defenses. Pitchers are allowed to throw only fastballs, either two seam or four seam, and they work on locations as well. The drill keeps your defense on their toes, and pitchers will realize that they can get guys out just on fastballs. You probably want to start playing this game in practice only after the pitchers have good control of the fastball inside and outside for strikes. All youth leagues ages 12 and under should make it mandatory that all pitchers can throw is fastballs because there would be so many benefits to this method.

Equipment

Baseballs   Field
Batting helmets   Bats

Number of Players

Full team

Setup

Nine players are on the field, and three are extra pitchers. On the other team, 12 players hit. A pitcher is always in the bullpen getting ready because after three outs pitchers rotate.

Procedure

1. After three outs, another pitcher of the same team goes in to pitch. He will already be warmed up in the bullpen.

2. A pitching change occurs after three outs. The other pitcher goes in again after three outs, just like in a game.

3. You judge how many pitches have been thrown and when another pitcher will take the place of one of the pitchers who has been pitching.

4. The defense stays on the field for 21 outs, which works on their ability to focus on each pitch for a long period. When they play 3 outs and in, it will be a lot easier for them.

5. After 21 outs, the teams switch defense to offense, and the game continues.

6. Pitchers are allowed to throw only fastballs, two or four seam, to any location. More baseballs are pitched in the strike zone, more balls are hit early, and the defense gets a lot of work. Finally, as pitchers move the fastball around, they start to recognize how many outs they can get with just a well-located fastball.

7. This drill allows the pitchers to work on their mechanics and control of the fastball.

Coaching Points

- The main point is to make sure that the pitchers are controlling the fastball well.

- Pitchers should be working quickly. They get the ball, get ready, and pitch. Hitters know that they will be seeing all fastballs; they just do not know the location.

- Start emphasizing to pitchers that they should first establish the fastball down the middle and see how many guys they can get out just on the fastball. When the top of the order comes back around, they can start spotting the pitches in and out. For the next time around the order, they can pitch up and down and so on.

51. Stride Position

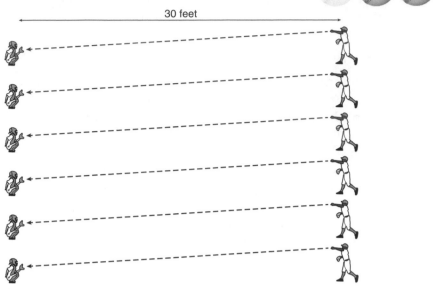

30 feet

Purpose

This drill helps pitchers feel and get comfortable in the landing position. In the landing position, the lead foot touches the ground completely. From the landing position described earlier, pitchers throw the baseball by working on gliding forward with the chest and head, rotating the hips, creating the Ferris wheel effect with the upper body, and bringing the elbows and hands together like a funnel. With this drill, they do not throw the ball hard at the start. As a result, they do not lift the back leg because they are not throwing the ball hard. When they are finished, the back foot should be on the toes, rotated with the shoelaces of the back foot facing down toward the ground. The strongest part of the body, which creates the most energy, is the lower part, and this drill teaches them how to use it properly. The chest should end up over the front leg, the head and eyes should be straight, and the throwing arm should be in the follow-through position on the outside of the stride foot.

Equipment

Six baseballs

Catcher's gear

Number of Players

12

Setup

Line up players as if they are playing catch. They should not be too far apart because they will not be throwing hard. The receiver can squat like a catcher to simulate a real situation. The players with the baseball get into a strong landing position. Check that the landing foot is pointing straight or slightly in and is not open. If the landing foot is not in that position, the players will not be balanced and will fall to one side.

Procedure

1. On your whistle, the players throw the baseball.
2. Check the finish to make sure that the hips are rotated properly, that the head is straight, and that good follow-through occurs.
3. The players who caught the ball then get into the landing position. This process continues back and forth on your whistle.

Coaching Points

- Make sure that players are in the proper landing position when they get ready to throw.
- Check that in the finish the back foot is rotated with the laces facing the ground.
- Check that the head and eyes are straight in the finish and that the upper body is forward and not straight up and down.
- Players should be in a balanced position with the lower body rotated and the upper body forward and not leaned to the side.

Variation

After the players become proficient at the drill, they should try to finish with the back leg in the air and balanced. This balance drill will help them learn to control the head, upper body, and arms.

52. Short Toss

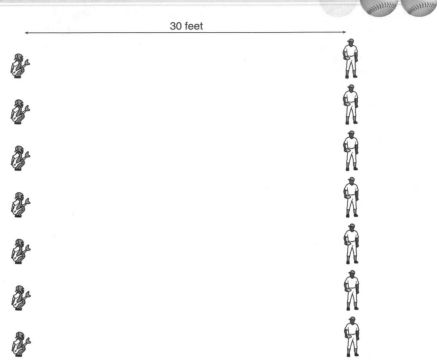

30 feet

Purpose

This drill gets players to work from a short distance so that they can focus on mechanics, not put stress on their joints, and learn how to throw the ball short and straight. The drill also allows pitchers to work on locating the ball by taking the front shoulder, head, eyes, and the hand holding the baseball toward the area of the plate where they are trying to throw the ball. Because they are at a short distance, they are able to focus on those things.

Equipment

14 baseballs

Catcher's gear

Number of Players

14

Setup

As in the other drills, line up the players about 30 feet apart if they pitch from 46 feet. One gets into the signal-taking position, and the other is in the catcher's position.

Procedure

1. When you say, "Set position," they go into the set position. When you whistle, they lift and throw.

2. After the catchers catch the ball, they work on transferring it out of the glove to the hand as quickly as possible. They should be working on this whenever they catch a baseball. They then become the pitcher and get ready to do the drill.

Coaching Points

- Watch for players to be smooth and continuous with the motion and not stop at the top when they get to their balance point.

- Watch how they control the baseball. Make sure that the ball is going straight.

- Use a smaller plate when you start. Instead of a plate 17 inches wide, use one 13 inches wide. You can make your own home plates by cutting them out of cardboard. Players then work with a smaller strike zone and increase it later as they become more consistent.

Variations

When the pitchers start to get good, you can call locations like inside, outside, middle, up and away, up and in, down and in, down and away, for strikes. The pitchers can be on flat ground; they don't have to throw from a mound. Using catchers allows the pitchers to work on location.

You can also use a wall with a box drawn on it for the strike zone. After pitchers master their mechanics and control, they can begin to work back toward the distance that they pitch from in a game. For example, if they pitch from 46 feet, they start at 30, then pitch from 40, and finally pitch from 46. They start from the stretch until they are comfortable and then do the drill from the windup.

53. Hitter and Catcher

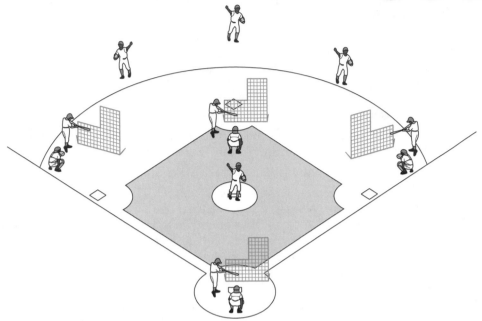

Purpose
This multipurpose drill gets pitchers accustomed to pitching to hitters and helps catchers work on things without having to catch the baseball. At the same time, hitters are working on tracking the baseball and identifying the pitch and speed. A pitcher throws to a catcher behind a screen, and the hitter is at home plate in front of the screen. The catcher gives the target and the location behind the screen. When the players have practiced this drill and are comfortable, you can remove the screen and have them do it live.

Equipment
Four baseballs

Four bats

Four helmets

Four sets of catcher's gear

Four screens

Number of Players
12

Setup
Set up four stations with three players at each—a pitcher, a catcher, and a hitter. Place a screen in front of the catcher.

Procedure

1. The pitcher pitches to the catcher; the ball will hit the screen.
2. The catcher places the glove where the ball hits the screen. The catcher works on holding the glove there for a split second so that the umpire has a clear view.
3. If the ball hits the dirt, the catcher drops to block it. Wherever the pitch is, the catcher reacts to it.
4. In the meantime, the hitter watches the ball from release to home plate. He works on loading by coming back and down with the front foot to balance.

Coaching Points

*   Watch for the pitcher's control.
*   Watch the catcher's ability to react to the pitch, frame it, and block it if it is in the dirt.
*   The hitter should be tracking the baseball and watching it all the way to home plate.

Variations

You can have the pitcher throw colored baseballs and require the hitter to call the color of the ball. Finally, you can take away the screen and have the pitcher throw. You can then have the hitter bunt so that the catcher gets used to having the bat in the way before he catches the baseball. This activity also gets the pitcher accustomed to throwing to a hitter.

54. Runner on First

Purpose

This drill teaches young pitchers how to hold the runner at first base while also throwing strikes. The drill uses many players and can be practiced in several areas of the field; you do not need a pitching mound. The pitcher has to do multiple things like holding the runner on first by throwing over to first or holding the ball longer than normal before throwing home.

Equipment

Plastic pitching rubber   Helmets
Plastic first base   Bat
Plastic home plate   Catcher's gear
Baseballs

Number of Players

15

Setup

Set up three stations of five players each—a pitcher with a baseball, a catcher in full gear, a hitter with a helmet on and a bat, a first baseman at first, and a runner at first with a helmet.

Procedure

1. The pitcher throws the ball over to first base two or three times so that he gets used to doing it. After three times, he throws the ball home or to first. If he throws home, the runner has to decide to shuffle twice, not go, and get back to first. If the runner decides to go, he takes two or three steps as if he were stealing and then comes back to get ready again. If the ball is thrown home, the hitter can take the pitch or work on his sacrifice or bunt for a hit. If the ball is thrown to first, the first baseman works on his tags.

2. The pitcher, in this case, does not lift the knee up high to throw the ball home if he is a right-handed pitcher. He lifts the foot up and back just an inch or two off the ground. He still brings it back a little to load so that it feels natural. He develops the same load but lifts the foot just a couple of inches off the ground.

Coaching Points

- Watch that the pitcher does not lift the leg up high if he is a right-handed pitcher. Lefties should not lift the leg high either.

- With a left-handed pitcher, make sure that the foot does not cross the rubber if he would like to go either to home or to first. If it crosses the rubber, the pitcher must go home.

- Watch how the right-handed pitcher throws to first base. He should use a quick hip turn in which both feet move just barely off the ground. The hip movement makes the feet move faster.

- You should also watch the first baseman to see that he tags straight down to the base and does not swipe.

- Watch how the runner reacts to the pitcher and whether he takes a good secondary lead or executes a straight steal.

- Watch how the hitter times the pitch and tracks it or how he executes the bunt. You can place cones down the third- and first-base lines to give the bunter a target. He tries to bunt the ball between the cones.

- Watch how the catcher catches the ball. If the runner begins to go, note how the catcher comes out of the squat into a good throwing position and how he transfers the ball.

Variations

If you have only 12 players, you can use 6 at each of two stations. The sixth player is the shortstop or second baseman. From his position he reacts and goes to the base to take the throw. If you want to get a little more advanced, you can use a stopwatch to time how long it takes your pitcher to throw the ball home to the catcher. Start the stopwatch when the pitcher's front foot lifts and stop it when the catcher catches the ball. In addition, time the catcher from when he touches the ball to when the player at second touches it.

With young players just practice the drill at first. Then, as they get better, you can time them to get an idea where they are with their times.

55. Land and Throw

30 feet

Purpose

In this drill the players move backward to the balanced position. After they get into the balanced position, pitchers should never stop their momentum, but in this drill they start stopped in the balance position. They start this way so that they can feel the position they should get to before they continue the motion. They also need to feel how to ride the back leg through the throwing delivery. Again, they do this drill slowly at a short distance.

Equipment

Seven baseballs

Catcher's gear

Number of Players

14

Setup

Line up the players as if they are going to play catch. Players in one line are in a balanced position with a baseball. Players in the other line are in a catching position.

Procedure

1. On your whistle, they throw the baseball.
2. From the balance point, they throw the baseball and get into a one-leg balanced position in which the back leg is in the air.

Coaching Points

- Emphasize controlling the body from balance to finish, especially the head and hand. The baseball should be going toward home plate.
- Check at the finish that they are completely balanced with the back leg in the air. This drill requires a lot of body control. The head should be straight, not tilted.

Variations

If the drill is too hard for some players, have them go from a balanced position to land, stop, and then throw from there. When they can control the land, they can put it all together.

Another thing you should do is have the players throw into a net or fence with their eyes closed. This activity will give them a great feel of the body. When players have their eyes closed, they have to feel the correct movement. After they get good at throwing with their eyes closed into a net or fence, they can try it with a catcher.

8

Baserunning Drills

Baserunning is a fundamental of the game that incorporates many facets that players can work on no matter what their running speed. Coaches of young players often do not work with their teams on this part of the game. Running the bases is an art. If coaches teach baserunning correctly, they will increase the ability of their players to steal bases and take extra bases. Fast base runners force fielders to throw to another base because the runner got there quicker than the fielder expected. In the field, faster players are able to get to and catch more balls. Before working on baserunning, coaches need to teach young players how to run properly and have them run every day to get faster. Speed and agility training is an important part of helping young players develop their athleticism. After a young player has developed his athleticism, all the facets of baserunning become a lot easier. Most of the time players cannot develop athleticism by playing baseball. This should be a priority when it comes to helping young players run the bases better.

To work on running and running the bases, your warm-ups in practice and before games need to be organized around running. Running needs to become a habit for young players. You can begin and end practices with fun running drills and games. Keep in mind that you always want to end practices with a competitive and fun activity because the last thing they do is what they remember. You want them remembering that practice was fun so that they learn faster.

Coaches should talk to track coaches to learn the proper running techniques so that they can help their players run better. Track coaches can teach the techniques and drills that allow players to perfect their running.

A few things need to be taught to help with all facets of baserunning. First is the ability to move quickly from one spot to another. This art is used in baseball and in many other sports. It begins with the hip turn, pushing off one foot and going. This turn will help runners and fielders. In this technique, players turn their hips as quickly as possible, keep the feet low to the ground, and turn on the angle that they need to run. The hip turn helps them move their feet faster. As they turn their hips and their feet touch the ground, they push off with the back foot. This turn can be practiced in warm-up drills, as we explain in the following drills.

Base Stealing

The base-stealing technique is the same technique that players use when they go for a ground ball to the right or left. In the ready position when they take the leadoff at first, the feet are about shoulder-width apart. The foot closer to second is slightly turned, and the hands are off the knees and in middle of the body. In using the foot closer to second base, players lift it slightly up and back, barely off the ground. As they do that, their weight begins to fall toward second because the foot is being lifted (it is not a step with the foot). At the same time they push with the other foot. Between the lift and the push, the body explodes toward second base. The players can practice this technique by doing it as a drill during warm-ups.

Another important facet of baserunning is for the hitter to have a balanced, controlled swing so that he can be heading quickly to first base. The hitter who has an off-balance swing cannot head toward first as quickly. For a right-handed hitter, the back foot (the right foot) begins to rotate, causing the backside to stay balanced or fall slightly toward the plate. As this happens, the right foot steps toward first after the ball is hit. When players hit the ball, they need to look where they hit the ball so that they can determine whether it is staying in the infield or passing through the infield for a hit. Hitters should run directly to first base until they recognize that the ball has passed the infielder. If that happens, they begin to head for the coach's box or take the angle. A coach knows when to send the runner along, but runners can react quicker and have better judgment when they decide on their own. At first, players will make mistakes, but as they begin to make decisions, they will become better at it. The players will also feel good about being able to make their own decisions when playing the game. After runners run past the bag and are safe, they look to see whether an overthrow has occurred. They can turn to either side to come back to the base. People often think that if the runner turns his body toward second, he has made an attempt to go to second and can be tagged out. This is not true. The key word is *attempt*; the runner has to take a step toward second, to attempt to go to second base.

The runner on first base needs to know several things before he takes his lead and decides what to do on the pitch. Now the base runner needs to get his sign from the third-base coach and keep his eye on the pitcher. As the pitcher gets his sign from the catcher, the base runner begins to take his lead. The lead will be a step with the left foot, a step with the right foot, and a turn. The feet never cross or come together. The lead can also be a few shuffles without bring the feet together. How far the runner takes the lead is up to him. Several factors determine the size of the lead, and the runner is the best judge of it.

In practices or practice games, players can take a longer lead than normal to learn their maximum lead. If they get picked off in practices or practice games, I allow them to stay on the base, but if they get picked off twice they are out. This rule helps players get a longer lead than normal so that they can explore their maximum ability. The leadoff position in baseball is called a primary lead.

What base runners do from first base and how they do it is important to their progress to the next base or bases. They have to work hard and be aggressive. After the pitcher lifts the front foot, he must go home with the pitch, so the secondary lead is extremely important. As soon as the pitcher lifts the front foot, the base runner must take an extremely aggressive secondary lead by shuffling without bringing the feet together. He shuffles until the ball gets into the hitting zone to see what happens with the hitter. Of course, he knows the number of outs, so he can decide what he will do when the ball is hit. Runners make mistakes by stopping after taking their secondary lead because they stop before the ball gets into the hitting zone. By then the catcher has a chance to throw the ball to first base. If a runner goes back hard all the time, it will become a habit. The catcher will see that he has no chance of getting the runner and will tend to forget him. The runner gains an advantage because now he can be more aggressive with his lead. He can come back to the base in several ways. One is by coming back to the back front tip of the base with the left foot and then swinging with the right to catch himself. This makes the first baseman go farther for the runner if he is trying to touch the runner at the waist or chest. We teach our runners always to dive back to the base, be aggressive, dive to the outside of the base with the right hand, catch themselves with the left, and then make sure to turn the head toward the outfield foul side of first base to see whether the ball was overthrown.

Another way to get back to first is for the runner to come back to the back of the base with the right foot, stop, and plant himself. If the first baseman is trying to get the ball, he will be blocked by the runner's body. This technique, which can be used if the runner comes back standing up, increases the chance that the ball will be thrown away. Runners should be diving back and being aggressive most of the time unless they have a short lead. Coming back to the base aggressively is important when runners are on first and second because runners at first often think that the defense is paying more attention to the runner on second. Consequently, they are not as aggressive. Runners should never be picked off at first because they get lazy.

Getting Picked Off

If the runner gets picked off, he has some options. Because he has already taken a step to second, the natural reaction is to keep going toward second at full speed. But he should make one adjustment. As he is heading toward second, he should read who is taking the throw and where. If the shortstop is taking the throw on the infield side, then the runner should try his best to get to the inside to take away the throwing lane. This location makes it difficult for the thrower if he does not get his body far enough inside. In addition, the receiver has a hard time seeing the throw. As the runner sees who is taking the throw and where, he heads for that person.

With a man on first and a ball hit to the outfield, the runner who had an aggressive primary and secondary lead has a better chance of getting to third base. Our team philosophy is that when an outfielder has to take a step or two on an angle to the right or left, we will be aggressive and take third. We teach players to be aggressive rather than tell them not to make the first or third out at third base because we do not want to teach defensive running. It has been traditional in baseball to teach defensive running because many believe that if you are cautious, you have a higher chance of scoring the runner from second base. Statistics do not support that theory. In the drills section we show you how to practice being aggressive so that in games you become more successful.

A runner on second base uses a similar leadoff by taking a primary lead and an aggressive secondary lead. He uses a slightly different technique than he uses for the lead at first. At first base he wants to be even with the base, but at second base he wants to be back slightly, forcing the shortstop to stay back and not get in front of him. By being back he can also peripherally see the second baseman. From this position the runner slowly begins walking on an angle toward third until he gets even with the base. He should time the walk to reach the base line just as the ball gets to the hitting zone. This technique allows the runner to get closer to third because of the angle that he is taking. From his viewpoint, the pitcher will not notice the extra distance gained by the runner. The runner will be moving as the ball gets into the hitting zone, not stopped. A way for coaches to show runners why this is a great way to take a lead and how they will gain some ground to third base is to place all the position players on the mound with a runner at second base. By being on the mound, the position players will see that the pitcher does not notice that the runner is gaining more ground. The runner wants to get even with the base line because the shortest distance between two points is a straight line. If the runners practice this technique, they will also be able to score easier on a base hit.

In taking a lead, the runner wants to take a short shuffle every time the pitcher looks home so that the pitcher does not see it. These small steps produce a larger lead, and the pitcher will not notice.

When the runner is on third, the leadoff is dictated by whether the pitcher is in a windup or stretch position. When the pitcher is in a windup position, the runner takes a shorter lead in foul territory because if he is in fair territory and the ball hits any part of the body while in fair territory, he is out. As the pitcher starts his windup, the runner begins to walk and tries to time either leg touching as the ball is in the hitting zone. Because he is moving as the ball hits the hitting zone, he will be able to react much faster. If the catcher catches the ball, the runner pushes off the lead leg and comes back in fair territory to block the catcher's throwing lane to third. He uses the same technique if the ball is hit in the air with less than two outs. He pushes off the landing foot and goes back to the base to tag up. The runner judges when the outfielder touches the ball and then goes. The coach does not tell him when to go; he tells the runner only whether he wants him to go or not.

The drills that follow are designed to help players learn how to be aggressive when running the bases.

56. Baserunning Game

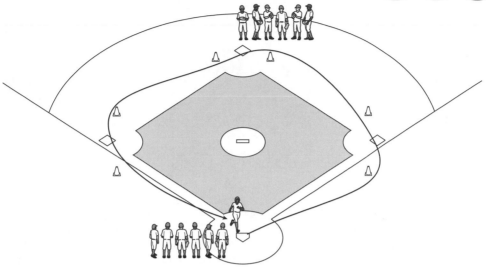

Purpose

You can use this drill at the end of practice for a fun game. Work on baserunning and make it a natural instinct. Plus it is competitive and fun for the players.

Equipment

Bases

Six cones or plastic milk cartons with water in them

Number of Players

Full team

Setup

Divide players equally into two teams. Make it fair by having the same amount of speed on each team. When you give them the order, mix them up. Don't place all the fast players first. Place half the team at home plate and the other at second base. Place a cone before and after each base. When the runners run around the bases, they go around the first cone and inside the second cone. This will help them understand how the bases are run.

Procedure

1. On the whistle, the first runner at each base begins to run around the bases until he gets all the way back to the base where he started. When he touches that base, the next runner goes.

2. The team to get around the bases first is the winner. You can play best of three or five, however you like. Winners get two baseball cards and the losers one.

Coaching Points

*   Make sure they run the bases correctly. If incorrect, send the runner back. Also, make this the end-of-practice drill because players will be warmed up.

57. Swing Bat

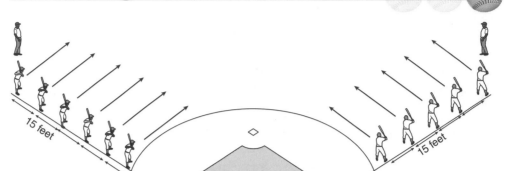

Purpose

This drill teaches young players how not to throw the bat after they hit the base-ball in a real game. We often tell players not to throw the bat, but getting through to them is difficult. In this drill you will also be teaching players how to control the body on the swing so that they are balanced and in a better position to run quickly to first base.

Equipment

12 Wiffle ball bats
Two cones

Number of Players

Full team

Setup

The players all line up down the outfield line, spread far apart so that no one can get hurt. They should be at least 15 feet from each other. If possible use a Wiffle ball bat when you start doing this drill. Players get into their hitting position.

Procedure

1. On your whistle, the players swing fast.
2. After they swing, they stop and freeze in the follow-through.
3. On your next whistle, they drop their bats, which will drop right behind them onto the ground.
4. On your third whistle, they run.
5. Have them run for or five steps, come back, and repeat the drill.
6. Now, on your first whistle, they swing and drop, but they do not run until the next whistle.
7. Finally, on one whistle, they swing, drop, and run. Ultimately, they will always swing, drop, and run.

Coaching Points

- Look for how good the follow-through is, all the way around. See that they are holding on to the bat at the end before they drop it.
- The players do not need to run 70 or 90 feet in this drill because they did it in the first drill.
- If a player still does not get it, he should stop and drop until he feels comfortable.

Variations

A coach on one knee can throw Wiffle balls to the hitter. The hitter hits and drops the bat. You can place two cones behind the hitter to mark out an area where he has to drop the bat. Depending on the number of coaches available, this drill can be done at each base, each of which can simulate home plate.

58. Warm-Ups for Baserunning

Purpose

You can use several warm-up drills that simulate various baserunning situations. You can use them before your baserunning work or daily as part of your warm-ups. To work on these drills, players first all line up even with an orange cone that represents first base. They will head to the next cone that might be 70 to 90 feet away, depending on the distance between the bases for your players.

Equipment

Two orange cones

Number of Players

12 to 14

Setup

Players take their leads all together on one line. They are about five feet apart, and they line up on the left-field or right-field foul line.

Procedure

1. All the players line up on the foul line. A pitcher simulates a pitch by getting into the signal-taking position, going to the set position, and then pretending that he is throwing back to first base. As the pitcher gets into the stretch, the players on the foul line simulate their leadoff. They take two shuffles and get their lead. When the pitcher throws over to first base, they work on getting back to the base.

2. Players do the same drill but take two shuffles and go. The pitcher simulates pitching to home. The runners take two shuffles and take off for second base because the ball is hit on the ground and they need to go or because two are out.

3. Players do the same drill, but now the ball is hit in the air. They get back to the base, and when the outfielder touches the ball, they go to the next base. So after the pitcher delivers the pitch, the players take two shuffles, come back to the base and tag, and then run to the next cone, which represents the next base.

4. Delay steal: Players do the same drill, but they take three shuffles and go. In this situation they are simulating a delay steal. By the runner's third shuffle, the catcher has normally caught the ball and is ready to throw it back to the pitcher. The runner is going by then, and it will be hard for the catcher to throw the ball to second base. The delay steal also catches the middle infielders off guard and out of position to cover the base.

5. Straight steal: As soon as the pitcher lifts the foot closer to home, the runners steal. They lift the foot closer to second just slightly off the ground and push off with the other foot to go.

6. Walking lead at second base: Players now take a lead as if they are leading off at second base. As the pitcher starts to get into his set position, the runners start to walk into and closer to the base line. As the pitcher delivers the ball, the runners take two shuffles and then come back.

Coaching Points

- Throughout all six drills you have a pitcher simulating the stretch, holding the ball longer, going home, or coming back to first base. Pitchers should be at both ends so that when the players run from one cone to the other, they have a pitcher ready to do the drill.

- You can also use left-handed pitchers. These drills allow pitchers to get work, and the activity becomes more gamelike.

Variations

Advanced teams can add catchers with equipment and a first baseman to catch the ball. Pitchers can throw baseballs in the dirt to see what the base runners do. They react on their own. Catchers works on blocking and recovering the ball after the block. After they catch a baseball, catchers go to their knees once. If they do it once, they have to do it a second time. See whether the players pick this up and delay steal. Players learn to read a situation on their own and make a decision.

59. Hold the Runner On

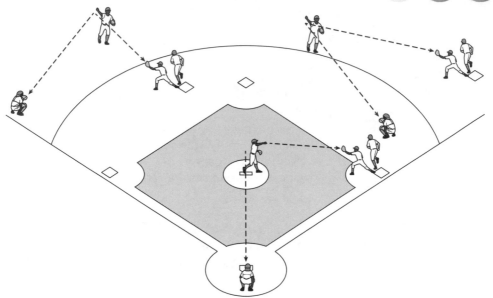

Purpose

This drill works on when the base runner should take off from first base in several situations, such as straight steal, ball in the dirt, and delay steal. This drill serves several purposes because it uses a pitcher, catcher, and first baseman to hold the runner. This situation occurs often in games. Many coaches assume that young players cannot handle it and just let the runner take second. If the players do not practice the situation, they cannot execute the steal or holding a runner on first.

Equipment

Plastic bases   Baseballs

Catcher's gear

Number of Players

12 players, 4 at each station

Setup

Set up three stations for four players—a pitcher, a catcher, a runner with a helmet, and a first baseman. Set up one station at home plate, one down the right-field line, and another down the left-field line.

Procedure

1. Pitchers get their signals and come to the stretch, and runners take their leads. Pitchers work on several things, such as throwing home after they set completely, waiting a few seconds after they set, going home, throwing to first, throwing home, and the ball in the dirt. All these situations could occur in a game. The runner reacts accordingly.

2. If the runner goes, he runs just four or five steps and comes back.

3. The catcher comes up ready to throw or blocks the ball and goes to get it, but he does not throw to second.

4. The catcher can also throw to first if the runner goes into a secondary lead after the pitch but does not go.

5. A runner who does not go works on getting back to first base.

6. The first baseman works on bringing the glove to the base to get the runner. If the pitch is delivered, he shuffles off the base to cover a ground ball.

Coaching Points

- Watch that the pitcher does not raise his leg high, as described earlier. The pitcher should vary his timing. He can count one-one-thousand and throw, to two-one-thousand and throw, or to three-one-thousand and throw. The pitcher varies his counts and does not always do them in that order.

- Watch the base runner to make sure that he reacts to situations properly and makes decisions based on what the pitcher or catcher does, thinking on his own.

- Watch the catcher to see how he blocks and comes up throwing, how he comes up throwing on a straight steal, whether and how he throws to first, and whether he goes to his knees after he catches. Watch the runner to see whether he reads the catcher going to his knees and then delay steals on the next pitch.

Variations

You can add players to simulate a game situation more closely. Add a second baseman or shortstop. He is not on the base because he covers second by coming in slightly from his position when the pitch is delivered. If the ball is not hit, he continues to move to the base. The catcher can throw down as he would in a game, and the runner can work on sliding. In this variation you need several runners so that one player is not running all the way to second every time. You can also use both a second baseman and a shortstop. One takes the throw, and the other covers behind him by taking an angle behind the base, not straight across.

60. Man on Second Reading the Coach

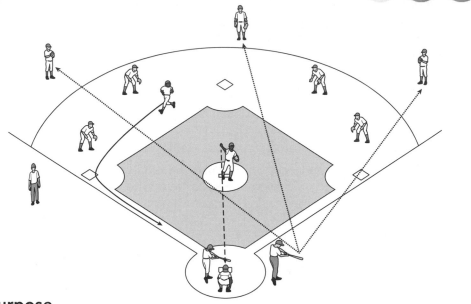

Purpose

This drill helps players learn to take a good lead at second base, be aggressive on their secondary lead, get a good jump, and read the coach at third base because the ball is hit behind the runner and he cannot see where it goes or what the outfielder does. On a deep fly ball, a runner at second may also decide to tag up. Scoring on a base hit from second base is unlikely if the runner does not get a good secondary lead and is not moving as the ball enters the hitting area.

Equipment

Three bases   Helmet
Baseballs   Bat
Catcher's gear

Number of Players

6 to 12

Setup

Place players at catcher, pitcher, first base, second base, shortstop, third base, and in each outfield position. Place a hitter at home plate with a helmet, tracking the pitches. Have a runner on second base

Procedure

1. The pitcher keeps the runner close to the base, and he can pick to second.
2. The pitcher delivers the ball to the catcher.
3. If the pitcher goes home, the runner on second, as he was moving in and over to third, takes his secondary lead.
4. As the ball crosses the hitting zone, a coach hits the ball to the outfield.
5. The runner picks up the third base coach to see whether he is to go home or not.
6. Our philosophy is for the runner to keep coming until the coach stops him. If the runner passes the coach, he keeps going, even if the coach yells, "Stop." If the coach stops him, the runner has to turn and sprint back or dive back. The coach tries to take the runner as far as possible to draw a throw so that the batter–runner can go to second base.
7. The batter–runner has to read the throw. After the throw passes the first baseman, if the batter–runner thinks that he can go on to second, he continues running.

Coaching Points

- Watch how the defense reacts.
- Watch how the runners react.
- If they do something incorrectly, you might want to repeat the play so that they feel the right way to do it. It is good to slowly review the play and then repeat it live.
- Watch for the first baseman who goes out too far to take the cut, giving an advantage to the runner because the ball crosses the first baseman sooner and the runner can go sooner. If the first baseman is deeper toward home, the batter–runner has to wait longer for the ball to cross the first baseman, making it harder for him to go to second.
- The defensive players work as they do in a real game.
- Sliding, tags, and relays all occur as they do in a game.
- Rotate the batter–runner to first. The runner on second becomes the hitter.

61. Reaction

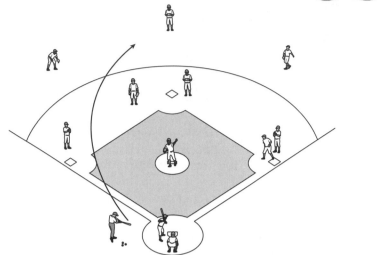

Purpose

I learned this drill from my mentor, ABCA Hall of Fame coach Dick Birmingham from Springfield, Missouri. The purpose is to teach the runner at first base to make a decision when the ball is hit directly to the outfielder and he either fields the ball cleanly or drops it.

Equipment

Three bases   Helmets
Baseballs   Bat
Catcher's gear

Number of Players

6 to 12

Setup

Place players at catcher, pitcher, first base, second base, shortstop, third base, and in each outfield position. Place a hitter at home plate with a helmet, tracking the pitches. Have a runner on first base.

Procedure

1. The pitcher on the mound delivers the ball to the catcher.
2. The pitcher keeps the runner close to the base and can throw to first to hold the runner.
3. If the pitcher goes home, the runner on first takes his secondary lead.
4. As the ball crosses the hitting zone, a coach hits the ball directly at one of the outfielders.
5. As the ball gets to him, the outfielder has two options: He can field it cleanly and get it back in, or he can turn the glove over and let the ball hit the glove and get away. Having the ball get away allows the outfielder to work on recovering it.
6. The batter–runner has to read the play and make a decision.

Coaching Points

- Watch how the defense reacts.
- Watch how the runners react.
- If they do something incorrectly, you might want to repeat the play so that they feel the right way to do it.
- The defensive players work as they do in a real game.
- Sliding, tags, and relays all occur as they do in a game.
- Rotate the batter–runner to first. The runner on first becomes the hitter.

62. First to Third

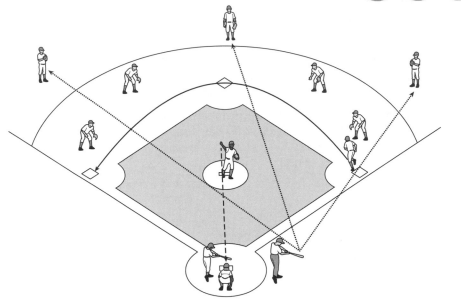

Purpose

This drill teaches players to be aggressive on their secondary lead, get a good jump, read where the ball is, and continue to third. As described earlier if an outfielder has to move to the right or left more than one step, the runner continues to third base. He will not be able to advance to third if he does not get a good secondary lead and is not moving as the ball enters the hitting area.

Equipment

Three bases   Helmets
Baseballs   Bat
Catcher's gear

Number of Players

6 to 12

Setup

Place players at catcher, pitcher, first base, second base, shortstop, third base, and in each outfield position. Place a hitter at home plate with a helmet, tracking the pitches. Have a runner on first base, a pitcher on the mound who delivers the ball to the catcher, and a runner at first.

Procedure

1. The pitcher keeps the runner close to the base. He can go home or pick to first.
2. If the pitcher goes home, the runner on first takes his secondary lead.
3. As the ball crosses the hitting zone, a coach hits the ball to the outfield.
4. The runner decides whether to go to third or not.
5. The defensive players work as they do in a real game.
6. Sliding, tags, and relays all occur as they do in a game.
7. The batter–runner stays at first. The runner on first who went to second or third goes in to hit. Players keep rotating.

Coaching Points

- Watch how the defense reacts.
- Watch to see how the runners react.
- If they do something incorrectly, you might want to repeat the play so that they feel the right way to do it.
- A common mistake is not running full speed all the way until the outfielder fields the ball cleanly and has the ball in his throwing hand. Most runners stop, assuming that the outfielder will field the ball or that the transfer to the throwing hand is easy. Fear stops most runners from being aggressive, so they must be encouraged in practice to take chances.

Variation

From this, you can let the hitter run as if he hit the ball. You go to the next phase of the situation, which is holding the runner at first if the runner gets to third or holding the runners at second and first. This becomes a baserunning drill as well as a defensive drill.

9

Rundown Drills

Rundowns are often practiced only occasionally, but players are expected to perform the skill under pressure during a game. Rundowns are difficult to accomplish because many players are involved in trying to tag an opposing player who wants to get away. Rundowns also involve a player running with the ball who has to throw it under control to a teammate. At the same time, the player with the ball has to know what the runner is doing and judge where his teammate is to catch the ball. All this occurs under pressure because if the player throws the ball away or misses the tag, the runner may return safely to the base where he started or possibly advance one or two bases. Then you have the player who is supposed to receive the ball as he moves or jogs forward to close the gap between the thrower and himself. He has the difficult job of moving forward while catching a ball, tagging the runner, and then coming up ready to throw to another base. In addition, after he throws the ball he needs to get out of the way to avoid an interference call. The rundown drills are a great warm-up.

Situations

Let's talk philosophy. A rundown can be executed in several ways. A lot has to do with what types of players you have and what they are ready to handle at the time. In addition, you will have your own beliefs about how the rundown should be executed. Let me tell you how we operate the rundown and why.

Runner Picked at First Base

The first thing to review is what the player who has just caught the ball does. Let's say that he just caught the ball from the pitcher at first base. What does he do now? This depends on what the runner does. If the runner takes off for second right away, the first baseman, who is most likely on the infield side, steps to that side, turns, and throws the ball to the shortstop, who would be on the inside part of the base. If the throw takes the first baseman way to the outfield side, he throws the ball to the second baseman. If the throw is right at the first baseman and the runner goes, the first baseman steps toward the pitcher to cut down the distance on the throw coming to him. This movement cuts the time needed to get the ball to second base. If the runner does not break immediately to second base, takes a jab step back (which is a natural reaction when picked off), but sees that he cannot get back, we now have a rundown. The first baseman runs at him hard to try to tag him, unless a runner is on third base. Then the first baseman runs a few steps at the player in the rundown and gives the ball to the shortstop or second baseman. At the same time, the shortstop or second baseman starts closing the gap, so the first baseman's throw is a short one.

Rundown Techniques

Depending on the types of players you have and their current development, you will have a philosophy about who decides when to throw the ball. We have the player running with the ball decide when he will throw it. The player with the ball has everything in front of him. He is calculating the runner's speed and distance, the location of the receiver, and his own running speed, so he can make a better decision on when to throw it. Our team knows that the player with the ball can fake a throw only once each time he has the ball, hoping that the runner stops and can be tagged. The receiver knows this and is ready for the throw.

Where does the player who threw the ball go after he throws it? He throws the ball and angles to the side that he threw to.

How many throws do you want to make as a defense, and do you run the runner back to the base he came from so that he does not advance a base if you make a mistake? The coach chooses this philosophy according to what he believes and where the players are in their development. We believe in being positive, and we view the statement "If you make a mistake, the runner does not advance" as a negative statement to our team, one that does not show confidence. We want to be an aggressive defense. I like to try to get the runner in one throw. Do the rundown well, be aggressive, and get the runner in one throw. We want to limit the number of times that we have to throw the baseball, especially if other runners are on base. To follow this philosophy, you have to practice the rundown technique a lot. We use the drills that follow as part of our warm-ups instead of running around the field to get warmed up. The following sequence of drills will help your players get better with rundown techniques. You can select a couple of the drills and include them in your warm-up process at the beginning of your practice or even use them at the end.

63. Running Hand

Purpose

This drill teaches players how to run with the baseball at a fast speed. This skill is difficult to accomplish because running while holding the ball up in the air at a 90-degree angle is not natural. Normally, when players run fast they pump their arms to keep the body in sync.

Equipment

10 baseballs

Four cones

Number of Players

10 or other even number

Setup

Line up players at the first cone. The players in each line run to the second cone. Players lift the hand, holding the ball up at a 90-degree angle.

Procedure

1. On your whistle, the players begin to walk to the next cone. You whistle for each line, and they come back as well.
2. Players turn around and get ready to go again with the arm at a 90-degree angle. This time they jog.
3. Next, players get ready and begin to run at half speed.
4. Last, players sprint.

Coaching Points

- See that players keep the arm and hand with the ball in it at a 90-degree angle the whole time.
- Players who are weak on the back side of the body will have a hard time keeping the arm up as they walk, jog, run, and run full speed.
- This drill develops strength on the back side of the throwing side because of the fatigue developed.

64. Running Hand Toss

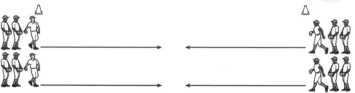

Purpose

This drill helps players learn to throw the ball on the run and, when they are the receiver, to catch it as they are moving forward. This two-purpose drill continues to teach them how to execute the rundown.

Equipment

Six baseballs
Two cones

Number of Players

12 or an even number

Setup

Have two lines of six players facing each other. Or have three lines of four players facing each other. The first guy in the line has a baseball. The players start about 60 feet from each other. Use two cones as a starting point for everyone.

Procedure

1. On your whistle, the player with the baseball begins to walk forward fast, and the receiver begins to walk fast toward the player with the ball.
2. As they get close, the player with the ball throws it to the oncoming player.
3. This continues because now the player who caught the ball continues to walk fast with the baseball held up and the next person walks forward fast.
4. This process continues until everyone has gone a couple of times.

Coaching Points

- Look to make sure that the players are walking fast as they do the drill.
- The player with the ball has his hand up, and the receiver has his hands out in front ready to receive the baseball.
- Look to make sure that the ball is not thrown too late or too early.

Variations

You can have the players jog and run toward each other. The player with the baseball can be in a jogging mode, and the receiver can be jogging or walking forward. The idea is to build from walking to jogging and to a full-out sprint in the next drill for the player with the ball.

65. Sprint and Throw

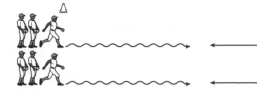 

Purpose

Now the players must learn how to throw the ball on the run and catch it as they are moving forward. Drill by drill, we are speeding up the process to game speed.

Equipment

12 baseballs
Two cones

Number of Players

12 or other even number

Setup

Have two lines of six players facing each other. Or have three lines of four players facing each other. The first guy in one end of the line has a baseball. This time the players are about 100 feet apart. Use the two cones as a starting point for everyone.

Procedure

1. On your whistle, the player with the baseball begins to sprint forward and the receiver begins to walk fast toward the player with the ball.
2. As they get close, the player with the ball throws it to the oncoming player.
3. This continues because now the player who caught the ball continues to sprint with the baseball and the next person walks forward fast.
4. This process continues until the players have done it a few times or when you decide to stop and start up again.

Coaching Points

- Look to make sure that as soon as the player catches the baseball he gets the hand up with the ball and sprints.
- Look to see that the players are throwing the ball on the glove side of the receiver.
- Look to make sure they are not late with the throw and that the thrower decides when to throw the baseball.

66. Throw and Tag

Purpose

Now the players must learn how to throw the ball as they are sprinting, catch it as they are moving forward, and perform the component of tagging the runner.

Equipment

12 baseballs

Two cones

Number of Players

12 or another even number

Setup

Have two lines of six players facing each other. Or have three lines of four players facing each other. You can also do this drill with six players in one line spread out and six in the other line spread out so that each player has a partner. The first guy in one end of the line has a baseball. Use the two cones as a starting point for everyone.

Procedure

1. On your whistle, the player with the baseball begins to sprint forward fast and the receiver begins to walk fast toward the player with the ball.

2. As they get close, the player with the ball makes the decision when to throw the ball to the receiver.

3. When the receiver catches the baseball, he has to secure it by having the ball and hand in the glove and tagging the person who threw the baseball.

4. The thrower becomes the runner after he releases the ball. He has to try to stop and go back before he is tagged.

5. If the thrower throws the ball too early, he has a chance to get back. If he throws it too late, it will be hard for the receiver to catch it and tag the runner, possibly resulting in a collision. So the thrower has the responsibility to throw the ball so that the receiver has time to catch it and tag him. After the receiver tags the runner, he comes up to throw as if another runner is on base.

Coaching Points

- Look to be sure that the players are throwing the baseball on the glove side of the receiver.
- The thrower should throw the ball on time so that he cannot stop and go back the other way before he is tagged.
- If the players do this correctly, you can have the fastest player with the ball and the slowest player receiving it and still get the out with one throw.
- Look for the receiver to come up ready to throw after tagging the runner.
- If the receiver does not tag the runner after one throw, have the players continue until they finish the play, but stress that the goal is to get the runner in one throw.

67. Pick and Rundown

Purpose

This drill teaches players how to catch the ball on a pickoff and begin the rundown. Several players are involved in this drill. The pitcher throws to first, the first baseman runs at the runner, the runner tries to avoid being tagged, and the second baseman or shortstop receives the baseball. The objective is to try to get the runner on one throw.

Equipment

Three flat bases   Three baseballs

Three helmets

Number of Players

Full team

Setup

Set up stations of triangles. One corner is the pitcher with the ball, another corner is the first baseman, and the last corner is the shortstop and second baseman. The players should be the same distance apart as they are on the field that they play on, but you can do these drills in the outfield.

Procedure

1. The runner takes a regular lead, the pitcher picks to first, and the rundown begins. In this case the runner takes a short step back to first, which is the natural reaction unless he was stealing. This makes the action more realistic.
2. The first baseman always throws the ball to the inside of the infield, in this case not on the glove side of the receiver, and the shortstop receives it there, while the second baseman takes second base.

Coaching Points

- Make sure the runner takes a step back to first before he gets into a run-down so that the play is more natural.
- Look for the first baseman to throw the ball on the inside of the field.
- Make sure that the first baseman does not run the runner all the way to second. He should run him a few steps and then get rid of the ball.

Variation

Give the runner the option of running to second base right on the pickoff so that the first baseman has to read that and get the ball to the shortstop right away. The runner can react either by continuing to run to second and sliding or by stopping when the shortstop catches the ball and getting into a rundown.

68. Three-Station Rundown

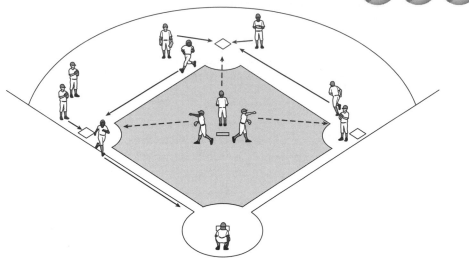

Purpose
This drill teaches every rundown situation for all positions.

Equipment
All four bases   Catcher's gear
Helmets   12 baseballs

Number of Players
12 or more

Setup
You have players at all infield positions. You use three pitchers—one on the third-base side of the mound throwing to third base, one pitcher on the second-base side throwing to second base, and another on the first-base side throwing to first.

Procedure
1. The pitcher picks the runner at first, and the rundown begins. The pitcher covers first base, and the second baseman works that rundown.
2. The pitcher on the second-base side picks to second. The shortstop catches the ball and begins the rundown toward third. You have two third basemen, and one works on this rundown.
3. As the pitcher throwing to third lifts his leg, the other third baseman goes to the bag. The pitcher throws him the ball, and the rundown begins.

Coaching Points
- Try to get the runner in no more than two throws.
- Each pitcher goes to the base to which he threw the baseball.

69. Four-Station Rundown

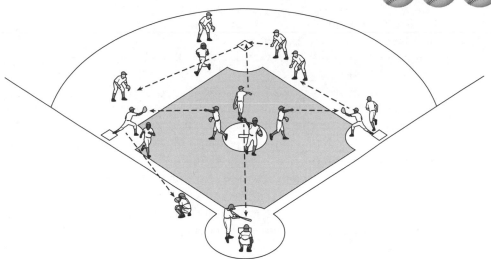

Purpose

This team drill uses all the positions and more, plus runners at each base. Every pickoff scenario is used in this rundown along with all the pitchers. This also allows for all the rundowns at each base to be finished.

Equipment

All four bases   Catcher's gear
Helmets   12 baseballs

Number of Players

Full team

Setup

You will have a full infield with all the positions. There will be four pitchers, one on the third-base side of the mound throwing to third base. One pitcher is on the second-base side throwing to second base and another pitcher is on the first-base side throwing to first. The last pitcher will throw home.

Procedure

1. The pitcher throwing to first picks the runner at first and the rundown begins. The pitcher covers first base and the second baseman works that rundown. Two second basemen are here; one takes the throw from the first baseman and the other works with the pitcher behind the mound on a pick to second.

2. The pitcher on the second-base side picks to second and the second baseman catches the ball and begins the rundown toward third. There will be two third basemen; one works on this rundown.

3. At the pitcher throwing to third lifts his leg, the other third baseman goes to the bag and the pitcher throws him the ball and the rundown begins with the catcher. There will be two catchers: one with the rundown to third and the other catching the pitcher throwing home.

4. The pitcher throwing home has a hitter at home plate, who can work on bunting. The pitcher can work on pitchouts with the catcher and also on sacrifice bunts.

Coaching Points

- Follow all the same philosophies, and try to get the runner in no more than two throws.
- Each pitcher will go to the base where he threw the ball.

10

Sliding Drills

I learned these drills from my mentor and friend Dick Birmingham, one of the best coaches I have been around in my 30 years in the game. He taught me a lot and opened many doors for me.

Sliding is not practiced much at the younger levels, probably because coaches assume that players know how to do it. On the contrary, sliding is a difficult skill that can cause serious injuries if not taught correctly. Proper instruction can help players avoid tags, get up quicker to go to the next base, and increase the chances of being safe.

Sliding is difficult for young players because they are going from an upward position and have to fall back under control, place their feet in the right spot to avoid injury, and slide on the butt area, which can cushion the blow of the slide because it's the softest part of the body.

Using the proper technique allows the player to maintain speed, lower the center of gravity, bend one leg under the other so that both legs do not go flying forward, which will produce more impact on the slide. The hands must be thrown forward slightly to keep the upper body up so that the head does not hit the ground. As the player slides, he throws his hands forward and places them by the ears to protect his face from the baseball.

Practicing this skill, if done correctly, can be fun. To get the hang of it and gain confidence so that they want to slide, players must practice sliding a few times a week.

Players can use several slides, such as the one used to avoid a tag, the pop-up slide, the fade away, and others. We will not show the headfirst slide in this chapter because it is can be dangerous for young players. The following sliding drills will help young players get to the point of doing the whole slide at one time.

Young players should avoid the headfirst slide because doing it wrong and hitting the chest on the ground can be dangerous. In addition, if players are not trained to close their hands, their fingers can be jammed or broken. Also, an infielder who jumps up for a thrown ball can come down on the player's hands. As players get older and gain more control of their bodies, they can begin to practice the headfirst slide. They should practice it a lot before attempting to do it in a game.

The first point in teaching the technique of sliding is to make sure that players run full speed when practicing. Then they have to emulate an airplane that is landing. They lower the center of gravity so that the buttocks area touches first, before the feet, which would be the front of the airplane. Tell players to begin their slide early rather than late. Sliding late can cause a major injury at the bag because the bag will not give but the body slamming into it will.

Begin with the first drills and build up to the actual sliding. Do not force players to run the first time and slide. Build their confidence in their technique and then have them work on sliding full speed. A good way to do this is to get a slip and slide, put water on it, and have players work on sliding in that setting before they practice it on the field.

The pop up slide is where players slide into the base with a bent leg and use it to pop straight up and go onto the next base. Sliding to avoid a tag is where you slide to the side of the base and reach with the hand closer to the base to hold on to the base. This is a more difficult slide and needs to be practiced.

70. Crawl

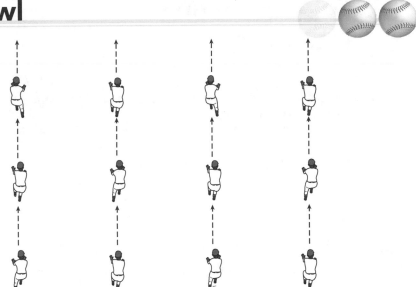

Purpose

To teach players which leg to bend under the other when they go into the slide and to begin teaching the proper position for sliding. Players start from the sliding position and work backward.

Equipment

None

Number of Players

Full team

Setup

Sit all the players on the ground on grass in the outfield. You can have lines or a circle.

Procedure

1. Have the players bend one leg under the other as they would when they go into a slide.
2. The only time they place their hands on the ground is now. As they are sitting on the ground, the players begin using their hands and start moving forward until you tell them to stop.
3. They then crawl back to the spot where they started in the same position, butt on the ground and leg bent. With the hands, they begin crawling back.
4. They switch legs and do the same thing.
5. Ask the players to bend the leg that they felt more comfortable being bent. They should bend that leg when they go into their slide.

Coaching Points

- Make sure that they crawl forward and back in a straight line as they would when they slide.
- Look to make sure that one leg is bent under the other the whole time.

71. Pop-Up Sliding Into Bases

Purpose

Several players at one time slide into a base, just as in a game, but now they get up and go to the next base. Do this team drill after you have had enough practices for sliding and know that everyone is confident in sliding abilities.

Equipment

Three bases on the field

Number of Players

Full team

Setup

Place three players with helmets on at each base: first, second, and third. A pitcher is on the mound.

Procedure

1. All players take their appropriate leadoffs. Have a pitcher on the mound, so the runners can work their leads off of him.

2. The pitcher throws home. The runner on first takes a secondary and goes; the same situation is at second and third. Each guy at the next base uses the pop-up slide and slide and then goes on to the next.

3. Keep repeating the process.

Coaching Points

- Make sure you take the right initial and secondary leadoffs.
- Watch how they do the pop-up slide. They should not place their hands on the ground; they should slide on their butts.

72. All Four and Slide

Purpose
To begin teaching how to kick the legs out and go into the slide.

Equipment
None

Number of Players
Full team

Setup
Place all the players in a line. Have all the players on their hands and knees.

Procedure
1. Ask players to begin crawling forward on their hands and knees.
2. As they pick up some speed, you yell, "Slide." From their hands and knees, the players kick their legs out forward and go into a slide position.
3. They kick the legs forward on the side that they feel more comfortable.

Coaching Points
- Make sure that the players crawl forward in a straight line.
- When they kick their legs, make sure that they go forward, not to the side.
- Check to make sure that they take the hands forward first and then put them by the head. The upper body should stay up a little and not fall straight back.

Variation
Have the players with their hands on the ground, their knees up off the ground, and their feet on the ground. From this position they begin to crawl forward and go into a slide.

73. Stand and Sit

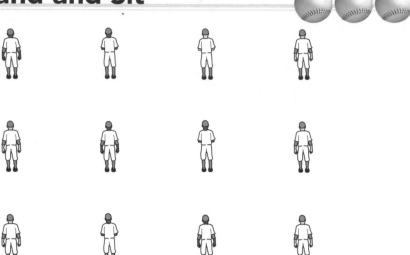

Purpose
To begin teaching young players how to lower the center of gravity, bend the nonbent leg, slide on the buttocks area, and place the hands in the right place.

Number of Players
Full team

Setup
Line up all the players so that they have plenty of room, about 10 feet apart.

Procedure
1. Standing up, the players bend the leg that they would bend when sliding behind the other leg. They will then be standing on one leg. They place their hands by the head in a half fist.

2. From this position, they slowly begin to bend the straight leg and lower themselves until they are sitting on the ground in a sliding position. In this way, they learn to lower the center of gravity and land.

3. As they go down, they throw their hands out in front to keep the upper body bent and to keep from leaning back too much.

Coaching Points
- The players should bend the leg so that the center of gravity lowers and they can more easily sit into the sliding position.
- Make sure that they sit down on their buttocks area, not on the side.
- Look to make sure that they do not reach down with their hands as they go to sit into the slide.
- Look to make sure that the players do not lean back too much and hit their heads on the ground. They need to keep the upper body bent and throw their hands in front as they go down so that the upper body stays forward.

74. Sliding Into a Base With a Coach

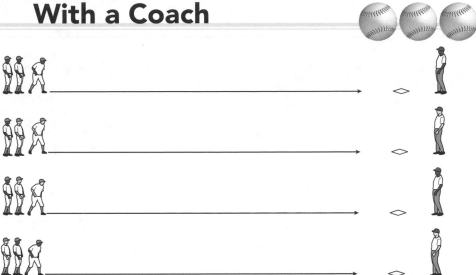

Purpose

To review all that the players have learned from the previous drills and put them together into a slide.

Equipment

Four bases

Number of Players

Full team

Setup

Set up the bases at the regular distance for your players' age. Have a coach at each base. If you have only two coaches, use only two bases. Players line up in front of each base and go one at a time.

Procedure

1. When the coach says, "Go," the first player in line begins to run and goes into a slide at the base.

2. After the slide, the player stays in the sliding position so that the coach can critique his sliding position and let him know what he did well, what he did not do so well, and what he can do better. For example, many players do not run full speed so it is hard for them to go into the slide.

Variation

To help players learn, you can replace the coach with a player and have that player critique his teammate's slide the same way the coach did. The coach starts, and then the player who slid becomes the coach. The player who was coaching goes back in line, and the process continues.

75. Game Sliding

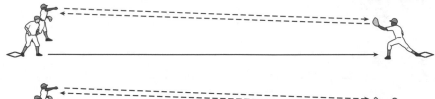

Purpose
Now we want sliding to be more realistic, as it is in a game. The player slides, and another player catches a ball and places the tag.

Equipment
Bases
Baseballs

Number of Players
Full team

Setup
The setup is the same as that used for the previous drill. You could have two to four bases and lines. Place a player at the base with a glove and a player where the runner is starting to run.

Procedure
1. Give the player at the base a baseball. This player throws the ball to the player by the runner.
2. On release of the ball, the runner can run. The player who catches the ball has to catch it and throw it back.
3. The player at the base catches the ball and works on tagging the runner. The runner works on his sliding.

Coaching Points

- Watch for all the techniques of throwing, catching, and turning to throw.
- Watch for the receiver to catch the ball and go to the base with the glove to tag the runner. He should not go to the runner's chest with the tag.
- Make sure that the receiver catches the ball first and then tries to apply the tag.
- The runner should be looking to see where the receiver catches the ball so that he can get to the other side and slide.
- Finally, you are looking to make sure that the runner slides early rather than late and that the technique is good. The runner should be able to pop up after the slide in case he has a chance to go to the next base.
- If the throw is bad and the ball gets away, the runner should pop up after the slide and take a couple of steps as if he is going to the next base.

Variation

Have a player at the base to act as an umpire and call the runner safe or out. His presence makes the situation more real and helps players understand how hard it is for umpires to make those calls. After a player slides, he becomes the umpire. The umpire goes to run, and the cycle continues. Also, after five runners, switch the thrower and receiver so that they can get in line to run.

76. Team Sliding

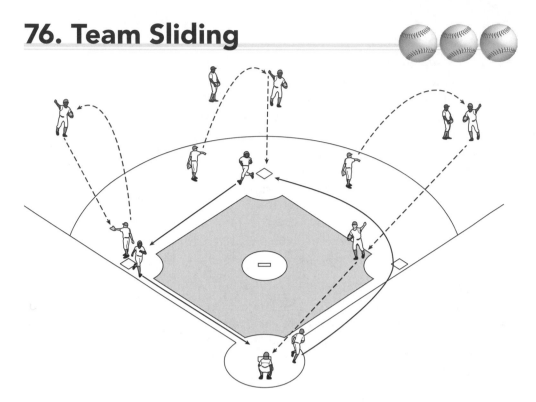

Purpose

This drill simulates several plays that would occur in a game and has the runners work on sliding.

Equipment

Baseballs

Bases

Number of Players

Full team

Setup

Set up a full field with a player at each position and a runner at home, second, and third with helmets on. Second baseman, shortstop, and third baseman have a baseball.

Procedure

1. On the whistle, the second baseman throws a fly ball to the right fielder.
2. The right fielder throws it to the first baseman for the cut home. The runner on third tags and slides at home plate. The catcher covers home.
3. The shortstop throws the ball slightly in the gap to the right of the center fielder (the throw is to second). As soon as the shortstop starts to throw, the runner at home heads for first, rounds it, and slides to second (the shortstop is covering the base). The second baseman can read the play; if the ball gets too far out, he can go for the relay.
4. The third baseman throws a fly ball to left field in foul territory and the runner on second tags and goes to third (he will slide).
5. This process continues.

Coaching Points

-   Watch how the relays are done.
-   Observe how players slide and whether they try to avoid a tag if they are out by a few steps.
-   These are all game situations, so see how they react.
-   The less likely to occur is the guy tagging from second to third but the ball is in foul territory so he can take the risk. Plus the important thing is that they are working on sliding, cutoffs, and relays.
-   Watch the runner go from home to second. Have the shortstop wait until the second baseman throws the ball so it gives them time to make the relay and the runner does not have an issue for when he rounds first. He can also be on first base and tag on a long fly ball to center field.
-   Make sure to stop the plays and review if something was done incorrectly.
-   The first time you do a review, do it one at a time so each player can understand what he did.

Variation

Add pitchers on the mound. You can have three of them, and they can work on backing up the throws.

11

Between-Innings Drills

In many games, coaches and players do what they have been taught to do or what they have been doing for years. Because we have a limited number of practices before the season and only so much time to practice during the season, we need to make sure that our players stay fundamentally sharp all the time. The things listed here are what you as a coach can do to use your time effectively during the game, especially between innings, to keep your players sharp defensively. We also offer some ideas on what to do with the players who are on the bench and not playing at the time. Having players sitting around doing nothing during a game wastes valuable time that could be devoted to player development. The time during the game can be used for players defensively between innings. Players can work on their swings when not in the game, or they can do things on the bench to continue the learning process. Players can coach the bases, with their helmets on, depending on the age level. All players should be doing something during the game. If players who are not playing are active during games, they will feel like part of the team, continue to develop, and be sharp when they enter the game.

For between-innings drills for defensive players, we do separate drills for outfielders and infielders and then combine them. For infielders between innings, the first baseman typically has a baseball and rolls it to the infielders, who throw it to first base. Most fielders field the ball in front of them and throw it to first base. This activity is good for maybe an inning because players need to work on baseballs hit at them. Then, for each successive inning you need to think about various plays that occur during a game and practice those situations. Examples would be working on baseballs to the backhand and forehand, fielding a baseball by dropping it and recovering, doing the same thing to the forehand and backhand, turning double plays, throwing on the run, and tagging third and throwing to first. To get more out of this setup, the second baseman and shortstop can use a second first baseman down the line, and the third baseman uses the regular first baseman. Mix it up as you wish.

Outfielders work on similar things—a ball hit at them and a throw, a ball hit over their heads, a line drive hit at them (the toughest ball), a ball to the side for a do or die. For each inning, practice a different play.

After players get good at those plays, you can work on the following:

1. The first baseman throws a fly ball to the right fielder. He throws it to the first baseman for a play at home, but the first baseman cuts the ball.

2. The second baseman or shortstop throws a fly ball to the center fielder. He throws it to the second baseman covering the base, and the shortstop backs it up. The play continues as if the runner is coming to second, and the second baseman works on the tag. The second baseman and shortstop take turns covering the base. One guy throws the fly ball first, and the other throws it the next time.

3. The third baseman throws a fly ball to the left fielder, and he throws the ball to the base for the tag on the runner.

The three preceding plays are turned into ground balls the next inning. These plays incorporate the outfield and infield between innings and have players practicing game situations instead of just playing catch, which is a waste of time.

77. Outfield Between Innings

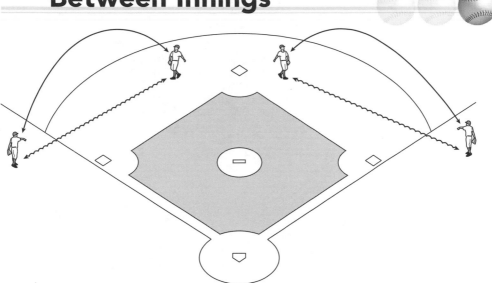

Purpose

Outfielders work on several things that they have to do in games.

Equipment

Baseballs

Number of Players

Four

Setup

You need a fourth outfielder working with the left fielder at the line. The center fielder and right fielder should be in their regular positions.

Procedure

1. Have the right fielder throw a fly ball to the center fielder. He catches it and throws it back to the right fielder. They change it up and throw fly balls and ground balls to each other.

2. The left fielder does the same with the extra outfielder on the line.

Coaching Points

*   Players should work close to each other so that the receiving player has to turn and catch the ball.

*   Players should throw the ball to each other over each shoulder. They work on their footwork so that it becomes second nature.

78. Ground Balls Between Innings

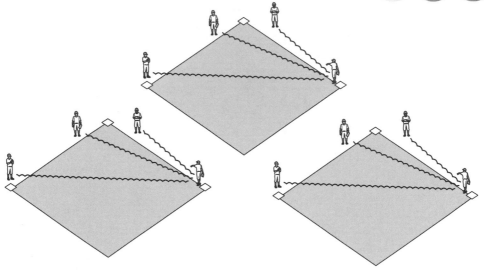

Purpose
To work on the various types of ground balls that occur in a game.

Equipment
Baseballs

Number of Players
Four per station

Setup
Set up an infield with a first baseman, second baseman, shortstop, and third baseman. You can do this on a normal field or in a grassy area where you set up the bases.

Procedure
1. The first baseman rolls baseballs to the infielders.
2. All infielders work on baseballs rolled at them, backhands, forehands, double plays, and balls that they drop and pick up.
3. On a field, you can have a group of four in the infield, four in right field, and four in left field so that everyone is working. You are also developing more first basemen. You will need three of them, and young players need to work on different positions.

Coaching Points

- Watch that players work on the proper positions and that they are creating game situations with each one.
- Make sure that the first basemen are receiving the ball properly and working on their stretch as they would in a real game on a close play.

Variation

You can split the team in half by having six running with helmets on and six in the infield. In this drill, you can use a pitcher and a catcher. A coach stands at home plate. If his hand is up with the ball, he will be rolling the ball out to a position player, the pitcher, the catcher, anywhere. If a ball is an easy one hop to a player or right to him, he has to drop the ball, pick it up, and throw it. If he fields a backhand one time, then the next time it has to be a different situation, such as a forehand. The drill starts with the hitter with a bat taking a swing. After the follow-through, the coach rolls the ball out and the play starts. The fielders finish the play, and the runner comes off the base if safe. The coach can decide to keep a runner on first to create a double play possibility. Again, if an infielder gets a one-hop ball, he has to drop the ball, pick it up, and finish the play. But if he already received and dropped the ball once, he can field it cleanly and finish the play.

79. Hitting During the Game

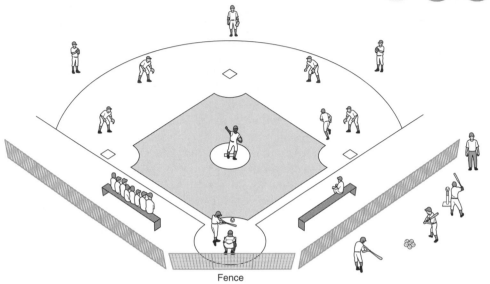

Fence

Purpose

To keep your players on the bench busy during games so that they stay focused. During the game, assign them things to learn. Then between innings, switch them to doing some drills.

Equipment

Bats   Batting tees

Wiffle baseballs

Number of Players

All bench players

Setup

Depending on facilities, you can have your players stand up between innings, go behind the dugout, and work on their swings. They can swing slowly if they are working on a technique and getting the body to feel the correct movement. You can speed it up to full speed so that they work on balance throughout the whole swing. They can get 5 to 10 quality swings per inning. You can alternate different hitters every other inning.

Procedure

1. If you have a fence or net, you can have a player toss Wiffle balls to a partner, who hits into the net. Again, you can get 5 to 10 hits per inning.
2. You can also have players toss Wiffle balls up on their own and hit into the net.
3. You can use batting tees, but you would need a tee for each player.
4. Players can work on their swings with no baseballs.

Coaching Points

- If you want players to work on the correct contact point, have them toss the ball up and take a half swing.
- You can also have players play check-swing pepper in an area where you have room for two fielders and a hitter.

80. Multiple Infield

Purpose

This drill covers several plays between innings so players stay sharp.

Equipment

Baseballs

Number of Players

Infield plus one more first baseman

Setup

Use a regular infield. The pitcher warms up with catcher. Two first basemen, second one will be down the first-base line toward home or can be past first base down the line if he is taking grounds from the shortstop or second baseman.

Procedure

Drill means the ball is being rolled. So drill 2 would mean the second ball is being rolled.

Drill 1

1. First baseman on the bag rolls a ground ball to the third baseman for a double play to the second baseman and then throws back to him.

2. Second first baseman down the line rolls a ground ball to the shortstop, who backhands it and throws it back to him.

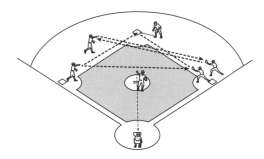

Drill 2

1. First baseman on the bag rolls the ball to the second baseman and they turn a double play back to him.

2. Second first baseman rolls the ball to the third baseman, who makes the throw back to him.

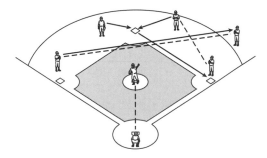

Drill 3

1. First baseman on the bag rolls the ball to the second baseman, who backhands the ball and throws it back to him.

2. Second first baseman rolls the ball in the whole to the backhand of the shortstop and he goes to third for the tag at third base. Third throws the ball back to the second first baseman.

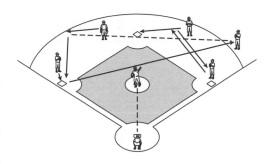

Drill 4

1. First baseman on the bag rolls a ball to the backhand of the second baseman, who steps on the base, fakes a throw to first, makes a full turn, and throws to third to get the runner making a long turn at third.

2. Second baseman rolls a ball to the shortstop, who drops the ball, picks it up, and makes a throw back to the first baseman.

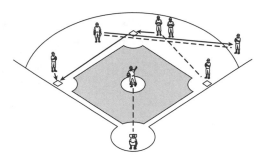

Coaching Points

- Players need to practice this before you implement it between innings in a game. So it could be a routine you use in practice to work on situations.
- The players get used to it and then it becomes a habit.

81. Assignments During the Game

Purpose

To have the players on the bench during the game be involved so that they do not just sit around waiting to go into the game. They are assigned something to do that helps them learn an area of the game.

Equipment

Three stopwatches

Two helmets

Three clipboards, three pencils, and paper

Number of Players

All bench players

Setup

You need three players, each with a clipboard, pencil, paper, and stopwatch. You can have fewer, depending on the ages, number of players on the bench, and what you think is important for that age group to work on while not playing.

Procedure

1. During the game, one player times the pitcher throwing the ball home from when the pitcher lifts his front foot to when the ball hits the catcher's glove. This player uses a stopwatch and writes down the times on a sheet of paper.

2. Another player times the catcher catching the baseball and throwing to second on a steal. As the balls touches the catcher's glove, the player starts the stopwatch. When the player at second base touches the ball, he stops the watch.

3. Two players on the bench coach the bases. They wear helmets, take signs from the coaches, and give them to the hitters. Switch the coaches every inning so that all the players learn the signs.

4. Another player times his teammates on steal attempts. He starts the stopwatch when the player starts running from his lead and stops it when he reaches second.

5. Another player is the fourth outfielder for the drills between innings.

6. Another player is the second first baseman for the drills between innings.

Coaching Points

- Have a coach on the bench helping the players who are working the stopwatches and writing down times until they get good at it.

- When changing players into a game, you have to assign the players coming out of the game to take the bench responsibilities.

- The main thing that these activities do is keep players interested and learning about the game. The times do not have to be perfect at the beginning.

82. Hitting Ground Balls

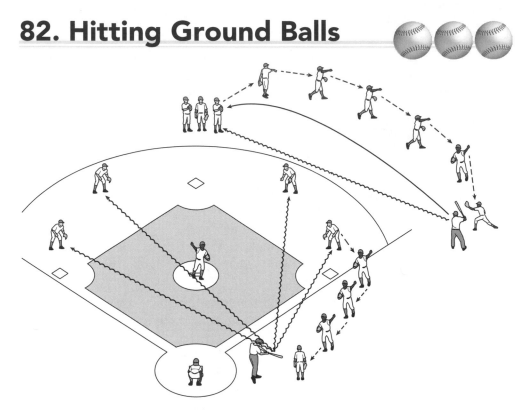

Purpose

To give ground balls to the infielders between innings so that they are getting them off the bat and from the correct angle. This drill is done during games between innings, but it must be practiced beforehand because it involves many moving pieces. This drill keeps more players involved.

Equipment

Baseballs	Helmets
Bats	Bases

Number of Players

Full team

Setup

All players assume their normal positions. A coach is at home plate with a few baseballs—one in hand and two in the back pocket. A catcher, if available, or another player catches for the coach. The coach stands on the right side of the catcher in foul territory. Three players line up down the first-base line in foul territory.

Procedure

1. To practice this first, you have your defensive guys in foul territory with your coach and extra players. When the coach says, "Go," the players sprint to their spots. As the pitcher takes his warm-ups, the coach hits ground balls to the infielders.

2. As soon as the fielder throws the ball, the coach hits the next baseball.

3. The first baseman catches the ball and throws it to the first player in foul territory, overhand, not underhand. He throws it to the next player. It's a relay so that the ball gets to the catcher with the coach.

4. If the ball is thrown over the first baseman's head, he lets it go.

5. After the pitcher is done, all the players come in as if they are going to hit.

6. The coach yells, "Ready," and everyone gets ready to go back out again. Now they just go to their spots, as they would in a game, with no huddle.

Coaching Points

- The main point is to practice this drill so that your players are ready to do it in a game. This drill can be substituted for infield work.

- You practice so that everyone knows what he should be doing.

- The player catching for the coach needs to have a couple of baseballs in his pocket in case of overthrows.

- In each inning fielders can create different situations.

Variation

As the infielders are doing their drill, another coach can hit fly balls and grounds balls from the left-field area in foul territory. The rest of the players can perform a relay from the outfielders. In this drill you can place all the outfielders in center field.

83. Infield and Outfield Between Innings

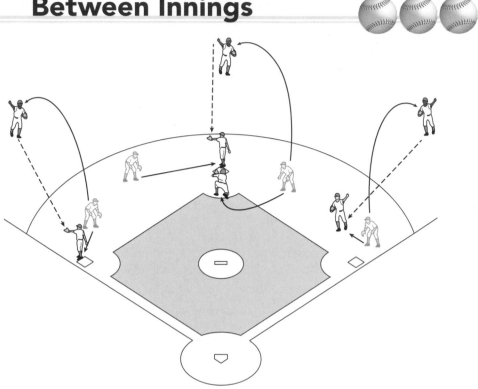

Purpose

To incorporate both the infield and outfield into game situations. You work on game situations between innings. After players get good at this, you can work on these plays during the game.

Equipment

Baseballs

Three bases

Number of Players

Seven

Setup

Players need to assume their positions just as they do in a game.

Procedure

1. The first baseman throws a fly ball to the right fielder, who throws the ball to first for a play at home. The first baseman cuts the ball and holds or fakes as if he is throwing home.

2. The second baseman or shortstop throws a fly ball to the center fielder, who throws the ball to the second baseman covering the base. The shortstop backs it up, as if the runner is coming to second. The second baseman works on the tag. The shortstop and second baseman take turns covering the base. One guy throws the fly ball first, and the other throws it the next time.

3. The third baseman throws a fly ball to the left fielder, who throws the ball to the base for the tag on the runner.

4. The three preceding plays are turned into ground balls the next inning. These plays incorporate the outfield and infield between innings and have players practicing real game situations.

Coaching Points

*   Look for the game situations to be done correctly, such as tags at the base, cutting the ball, and turning to the glove side.
*   Make sure that players go from fly balls to ground balls.
*   Have the outfielders drop a ground ball, recover, and make the throw.

12

Situational Drills

This chapter is important because many players can accomplish certain fundamentals in practice when pressure is absent but then seem to struggle in game situations. As coaches, we need to figure out how to put the fundamentals into gamelike situations in practice so that players develop habits that they can execute in games. Coaches often practice various game situations but do not incorporate the pressure that would occur in a real game. In this chapter we show you how to practice game situations under real game pressure. Players will become more successful in real games, although errors will always occur in games. You are trying to minimize errors by practicing real game situations.

84. Relay

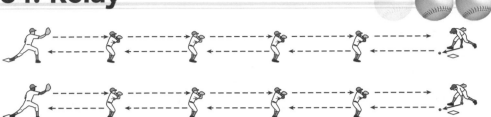

Purpose

To work with players on relaying a baseball from one player to another so that they are able to throw out a runner advancing to another base. They may eventually do so well at throwing and catching that they are able to get two runners.

Equipment

Four baseballs
Four plastic bases

Number of Players

Full team

Setup

Form two lines of six players. The spacing between players depends on the age group. When you first start practicing this activity, use a distance at which they can accomplish it well. Increase the distance as they improve. Ultimately, the players will be in line working a relay drill. Have a plastic base by the first player, who is getting ready to throw the ball, and one base by the last player, who is receiving the throw. Each line has a player at one end of the line as the starter. He has a baseball placed on the ground in front of him. His hands should be on his knees so that he is ready to pick up the ball when the whistle blows.

Procedure

1. After you say, "Ready," and blow the whistle, the player with the baseball picks up the ball from the ground and throws it to the next player in line. The relay continues until the last player gets the ball. He starts the ball on the return trip to the player who started with it. The players then stop.

2. Players need to catch the ball on the glove side, turn to that side because it is quicker, and then throw it to the next player. Emphasize technique at first. Players should go slow and practice. As they get better, they can begin to speed it up, but they should stay under control because you want good throws. The throws should be right at the player's glove side so that he can just turn to that side and throw. The receiver needs to begin to turn to the glove side as the ball is coming. He does not catch it first and then turn. The players need to read the throw and anticipate where it is going. They move their feet so that they can catch the ball on the glove side as they are turning to throw.

3. As they get better at this, you can make it competitive by playing a game to see which line can throw it down and back first. If an overthrow occurs, the players have to throw it back to the person who was supposed to catch it. If a player turns to the wrong side, he has to throw it back to the person who threw it to him before continuing. If they continue and finish, they are disqualified.

4. Eventually you can play best of five and see who wins.

Coaching Points

- Watch that the players turn to the glove side as they are about to catch the ball.
- The momentum of the player catching should be going toward the next player in line.
- Players should catch the baseball with two hands and work on the transfer.

Variation

The first player throws the ball to the second player. The second player turns, fakes a throw to the third player, and then turns all the way around and throws it back to the first player. The first player catches the ball, turns all the way around, and throws it to the third player. The third player does the same thing and throws it to the second player, who does the same thing and throws it to the fourth player. He throws it back to the third player, who throws it to the fifth player, who turns and throws it to the fourth player, who throws it to the sixth player, who turns and throws it to the fifth player, who turns and throws to the sixth player to end the sequence.

85. Three and Four Relay Game

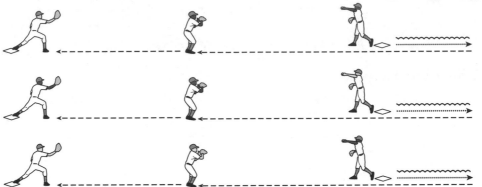

Purpose

By using three and four players in each line, this drill is more advanced and more gamelike. The person with the baseball rolls it behind him and goes to get it, as if a ground ball got by him. The player in the middle has to adjust depending on the player's arm and how far the baseball was rolled and move forward for the relay. He catches it and throws it to the next player, who catches it and places a tag at the base. Now the player who placed the tag starts the drill by throwing the ball up in the air, catching it, and throwing it to the relay player. The relay player can catch it and relay it or let it go through to the base if it is on line.

Equipment

Bases
Baseballs

Number of Players

9

Setup

Have three lines of three players to start the drill. The guy at the end of line has a baseball.

Procedure

1. The first player begins by throwing the ball behind him, getting it, throwing it up, and catching it as he would a fly ball.
2. After he catches the ball, he throws it through the cutoff man.
3. If the throw is accurate, the cutoff guy lets it go to the next guy, who catches it and places a tag.
4. The drill now starts from the other end and goes the other way.
5. After a few times, rotate the three guys so that the guy in the middle gets a chance to throw and tag.

Coaching Points

- You are looking for the correct fundamentals of throwing and making sure that the players throw through the cutoff guy. If he relays the ball, make sure that he turns to the glove side.

- When the player catches the ball, he needs to place the tag down in front of the base with the back of the glove, not the open part of the glove, facing the runner, to avoid exposing the baseball.

- Whenever the ball is thrown too far left or right and not on line, the relay guy should automatically cut the ball off.

Variation

Another way to do this drill is to have the player in the middle start with the baseball. He throws a fly ball at the player or over his head, or a ground ball to the player or to one side. When the player fields or catches the ball, the relay begins and continues until the tag is applied. This drill creates many situations and players need to line up and communicate in each situation. The players create and think on their own.

86. Four Man Relay

Purpose

This important drill simulates the ball that gets past the outfielders. The shortstop and second baseman have to go out for the cut and communicate. When they go out, the man behind will be about 10 to 15 feet behind his teammate and slightly to the side so that he can read whether the throw is too high or too far to the side. He also can be looking back to see where the runner might be.

Equipment

Bases
Baseballs

Number of Players

12

Setup

Have three lines of four players. Two guys are in the middle of each line. These guys are your relay and communication guys.

Procedure

1. Simulate a play like a ball that passes the perimeter of the outfielders and is an automatic double. Both guys then go out.

2. One is the relay guy, and the other communicates where to throw it. If the ball is too high, then the second guy tells the relay man, "I have it," and takes the relay.

3. In this drill, the person with the ball has to roll it far behind him so that he has to go get it as if it were in the gaps of the outfield. The players in the middle need to look back to see where the receiver is so that they can help line up the throw.

4. The backup guy performs various actions like holding the ball and not throwing, letting the ball go through, or relaying the throw.

Coaching Points

- In this drill, focus on the two players in the middle to make sure that they are communicating, that one is taking the cut, and that the other is backing up and lining up his partner so that he is in a straight line.
- Also, at times the second player might yell, "Hold," so no relay occurs. Treat this like a real game. The backup guy can make up certain situations like hold or relay.

Variation

The receiver can move so that he is in a different location. The backup guy has to locate his partner, line him up, and then make the call. This is like throwing to a different base than originally intended.

87. Multiple Outfield Infield

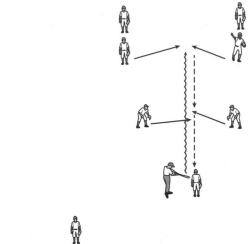

a

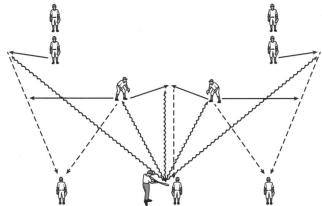

b

Purpose

This drill can be used to practice cutoffs and relays. Several players are doing things that relate to game situations. This drill can be used in practice or as a warm-up before a game. It can incorporate outfielders' communication, infielders' relays, ground balls, fly balls, pop-ups, line drives to the infield or outfield, and other things in one drill. You need only one coach with a bat hitting fly balls, ground balls, and line drives. This drill requires players to think on their own, make decisions, develop instincts, and work on game situations.

Equipment

One bat
10 baseballs

Two flat bases
Catcher's gear

Number of Players

Full team

Setup

Have two sets of outfielders, one on the right and one on the left. Have the same thing in the infield, two sets, one on the right and one on the left. You can have three players on each side. The next group on each side of the coach is the catchers, who can be in their gear taking throws and working on tags.

Procedure

1. One player stands next to the coach who is hitting. When a catcher catches a baseball, he tosses it to that player who gives it to the coach. The coach places his hand behind him without looking back. The player then places the ball in the coach's hand. This procedure allows the coach to focus on what the players are doing and get ready to hit the next round. After the players become comfortable, you can get lots of work done.

2. Now that everyone is set up, the coach shows the two infielders what can happen. If they get a ground ball up the middle, they need to communicate who gets it. One guy goes in front, and the other goes behind (a). The ball can be hit to the side of either guy or right at one of them. If the ball is hit to one side of the infielder, he fields it and throws it to the catcher on that side. If the ball is hit directly at an infielder, he throws it to the catcher in front of him. If the ball is hit in the middle, the infielder throws it to the player catching for the coach. The hits can be line drives, ground balls, or pop-ups.

3. Now the coach can hit a fly ball to the outfield. The two players have to do the same thing that the infielders did—communicate who will take it. If the ball is hit in the middle, the two infielders become the relay guys. If the ball is hit deep, they both go out. The guy catching for the coach is the final catcher; he will also adjust if he needs to move up. The coach can simulate all game hits.

4. The coach can now show another variation, the ball hit to the outfielder on the right or left, at the player, or to his side. This throw goes to the infielder on that side. He becomes the relay. Depending on how hard the ball is hit, he goes out, stays, or comes in.

5. After the coach has gone through all the variations, he can begin to start hitting balls to different areas. He starts slowly by hitting a grounder up the middle. As he does this, he hits a fly ball to the right. He lets the infielder throw the ball in before he hits again. Again, he goes slowly at the start to let the players get comfortable. Eventually, he will be hitting balls to the left over the fielder's head, a ground ball to the right of an infielder, a fly ball to the right, a fly ball to the middle, a line drive to the middle that the infielders try for, a liner to the right fielder, a ground ball to left that maybe gets by so that the outfielder needs to rush in to field it and throw it all the way. The catcher catches it and places a tag.

6. If the drill is done correctly, you can use four outfielders, two on each side; two infielders, one on each side; two catchers, one on each side; and one player catching for the coach (b).

(continued)

Coaching Points

- When you first start doing this drill, take it in phases so that everyone knows what he is supposed to do. Then, when they are comfortable, the ball can be hit anywhere. As the players begin to understand the procedure, the coach can hit multiple baseballs to create different situations at one time.

- One coach can be hitting, and other coaches can be on each side watching the catches, relays, and so on. They observe the fundamentals like the relay guy turning to the glove side, type of throw, tags, communication, and more.

- At first, you need to walk through this drill with your players. Line them up in their positions, hit a ball, and walk through what that group is doing. Do the same with the next group.

- This drill can be done entirely in the outfield. The coach can position himself on the right-field line and hit to center.

Variation

You can add a second coach to hit to the infielders and another to hit to the outfielders, but you really have to watch where each one is hitting. Timing is important to keep things going.

88. Infield Outfield

Purpose
This drill simulates practice before the game when a team is allowed to take ground balls and fly balls. It includes fundamentals used in a game.

Equipment
Baseballs

Number of Players
Full team on a field (two players can be at several positions if desired)

Setup
Players are at each position. A coach has a bat and baseballs; the catcher catches for him at home. The pitcher is on the mound.

Procedure
1. The coach does not tell the players where he is hitting the ball. He can lay a bunt down and the players have to make the play. He can hit to first baseman or anyone else to mix it up.

2. The only thing the coach can say is no one out or one man out on first. These are all situations players have to react to.

3. As this is going on, the outfielders are in short center field and coach on the left-field line hits them fly balls, grounds, and line drives. The outfielders throw the ball to a relay guy, who throws it in to the player catching for the coach.

4. After the infielders are finished, the outfielders get ready. The coach now hitting is by the mound and he has a catcher with him. He now hits different situations to any of the outfielders.

5. As this is going on, another coach at home hits ground balls to the first baseman, who throws home so the catcher works on tags. Or he lays a bunt down and the catcher throws to first base. You can do this because the first baseman is not being used when the first round is hit to the outfield. Most throws are going to second or third.

6. The coach at the mound comes home to hit, and most of the balls are plays at home.

Coaching Points
- Most coaches begin with the outfielders, but we start with the infielders while the outfielders get warmed up.
- Watch for correct execution of all the fundamentals and correct errors.
- Change up the sequence so players aren't able to anticipate when balls will be hit their way.

89. First to Third

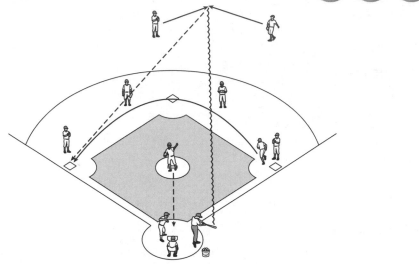

Purpose

This drill works on several things that pertain to game situations, such as runners' instincts to take an extra base and the reaction by the defense. It also teaches the defense in game situations because it includes real runners who run and slide. Of course, runners are working on sliding in game situations. Do this drill as you get closer to the season, perhaps a month before it begins, depending on how many practices you have altogether.

The runners in this drill have the goal to take third on any baseball hit to the outfield when the outfielder has to take a step or two to the left or right or does not hustle in to get the baseball. This drill teaches players to be aggressive, and they will see that they can take extra bases more often than they think. The drill also places a lot of pressure on the defense because they must field the ball cleanly, transfer it to the throwing hand, throw it accurately, catch it, and tag the runner. These skills are difficult to do in succession but even harder to do under real game conditions with real runners. The drill teaches the defense how to deal with this pressure, get the runner out, and prevent the batter–runner from taking second.

Equipment

Bat for the coach
Baseballs
Three bases

Helmets
Catcher's gear

Number of Players

10 or more

Setup

Set up players in the outfield. Put players at all positions. Put a coach at home with a bat. Have runners at home and runners at first with appropriate leads. Have a pitcher on the mound holding the runner if your league uses leadoffs. Have a catcher at home with a hitter.

Procedure

1. The pitcher throws home to the catcher and gets a chance to work on pitches with a hitter standing in with a helmet on. The batter does not swing.

2. When the ball crosses the plate, the hitter starts to run. The coach hits a baseball to the right or left of the left fielder, making him take a step to his left or right. The real situation is on.

3. The coach can hit anywhere in the outfield, so the players have to communicate and work on cutoffs and relays.

4. Runners must run hard and slide.

5. You can have a point system in which each time a runner gets third, that team gets a point. If the defense holds them, they get a point.

6. If you do not have enough players, use only one or two outfielders.

Coaching Points

- Make sure that your runners always wear helmets.
- The objective here is to get a runner into scoring position at third base, hope that the defense throws to third, and have the runner on first take second on the throw.

Variation

When the ball is hit right at them, your outfielders should occasionally drop the ball by letting it hit the glove and bounce off. They do this to see whether the runner is running hard, watching the play, and then reacting to the situation. Also, have runners go on any hit ball to the outfield to force the throw and if they are out they are allowed to go back to first base. The reason for this is that they will see that even on routine ground balls to the outfielders that they have a chance. Plus it makes your outfielders get the runner because many times we have to wait for this situation to happen to actually practice it.

90. Infield Pressure

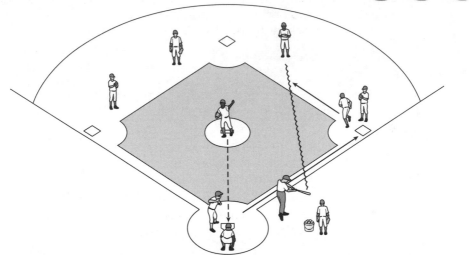

Purpose

This drill helps your players work under pressure by taking ground balls and getting the runners out. Again, these are real game situations that are not practiced enough but need to be accomplished during games. This drill also provides good conditioning for the runners and work on their baserunning. It teaches the defense always to finish the play in a game because they do it in practice.

This drill allows the defense to work on throwing to bases and pickoff plays so that the runners cannot take big leads that allow them to get to the next base quickly.

Equipment

Two bats

All four bases

Full infield

Catcher's gear

Helmets

Number of Players

Full team

Setup

Have a regular infield, including a pitcher, batter at home without a bat, and a coach hitting ground balls. Place your players in the infield. Have a catcher in full gear.

Procedure

1. The pitchers throw a pitch.
2. A coach hits the ball when the ball crosses the plate.
3. The hitter runs after the ball crosses the plate.
4. The defense works on getting the runner or runners.
5. If you have a runner on base, the pitcher and defense must keep him close to the base so that they have a chance to get a force play or turn a double play. They do this by throwing over to the base and working on pickoffs.

Coaching Points

- Look to see that the players are performing all the defensive situations correctly. When they do not do something correctly, stop the practice. Go over the play. Review it live but at a slow pace so that the players can absorb the idea. Then run the play again. Players must have a chance to run through a situation slowly before they do it full speed.

- Look to be sure that runners are running the bases correctly. They should run to first hard and straight. After passing the base, they slow down and look right but do not turn right. If an overthrow occurs, they just push off and go to second, doing all the things taught in the chapter on baserunning.

- For the first couple of times, have the coach hit a ground ball. The defense tries to get the runner out at first. Then have a runner on first and see whether the defense can turn a double play. Then open it up and allow the runners to do whatever happens in the situation, as in a real game.

- If a player reaches base, he stays there and play continues.

- When the coach hits a ground ball, the defense finishes the play until the end, no matter what happens. On an overthrow, they finish the play. The catcher needs to back up first base, and all the players finish the play.

- If you do not have any runners, have a coach with a stopwatch time the situation. The average runner in the major leagues gets to first base in about 4.2 seconds, so you can use that time for a ground ball and a double play. The coach or player starts the watch when the ball is hit.

91. Multi-Infield

Purpose

Create as many defensive infield situations as can occur in a game.

Equipment

Baseballs
Catcher's gear

Number of Players

Full infield

Setup

Place all your infielders at each position, including pitcher and catcher.

Procedure

1. Call drill 1. Review it and do a dry run so everyone knows what to do. Then say go. Keep doing the drill until you tell them to stop and then do drill 2 and so on.

Drill 1

1. Pitcher from the stretch throws a pitch to the catcher. The coach on the first-base side of home plate hits a ground ball to the first baseman, and the pitcher who threw the pitch covers first.

2. Catcher who received the pitch comes out throwing down to second as if a runner is stealing. Shortstop and second base cover and make the tag.

3. The coach on the third-base side of home plate hits a ground ball to the third baseman and he throws home to the catcher. Catcher applies a tag and comes up as if he is throwing to first base but does not throw the ball.

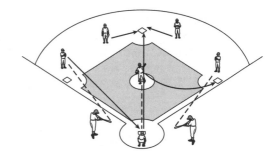

Drill 2

1. Pitcher pretends to deliver a pitch.

2. Coach on third-base side rolls the ball out like a bunt down the third-base line. Third baseman, pitcher, and catcher go after it and make the play to first base.

3. Coach on first-base side hits a grounder to shortstop and they turn a double play. A second first baseman down the line takes the throw; he should be closer to second base so he is not in line with the throw from the catcher to first in case there is an overthrow. Or put a screen between the two first basemen.

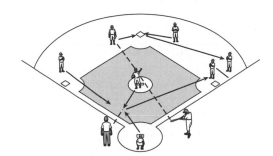

Drill 3

1. Coach on third-base side hits a slow roller to third and has to come in and make the throw home on the run.

2. Pitcher pretends to pitch home. Coach on first-base side hits a ball back at him and he turns the double play to second base and to one.

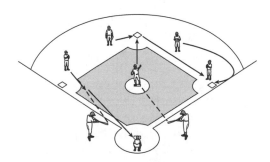

Drill 4

1. Coach on first-base side hits a ground ball to third baseman. Third baseman throws to second for the force and the second baseman throws home and the catcher applies the tag.

2. Coach on third-base side hits a ground ball to the shortstop and he makes the play to first base.

(continued)

Drill 5

1. Coach on the first-base side hits a slow roller to third, and the third baseman comes in on the run and throws to first base.

2. Pitcher throws a pitch home. Catcher throws to second, but the shortstop or second baseman come in and cut it and throw the ball home for a tag at the plate, simulating a first and third double steal.

3. Made sure the third-base play goes first so there is no interference.

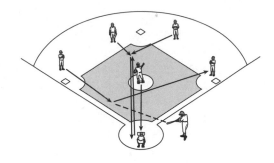

Drill 6

1. Pitcher has the ball and pretends there are men on first and third. Man on first breaks for second. The team yells for the pitcher to step off; pitcher looks at third to freeze the runner and then heads for the runner between first and second. Pitcher throws the ball to the shortstop and the shortstop runs the runner back to first and throws the ball on the run to the first baseman.

2. A coach behind the catcher rolls a ball out in front, down third, or down first. Catcher comes out and makes the play to third base, a force play.

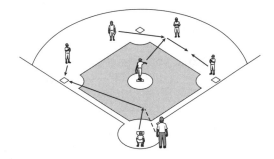

13

Player Evaluation Drills

If I were to put a 25-foot-long two-by-four piece of wood on the floor and ask you to walk along it, many of you would not have a problem doing that. But if I were to put the two-by-four between two supports 50 feet in the air, I think that many of you would have a problem! The odd thing is that the skill would remain the same. The only thing that would have changed is your level of anxiety or level of arousal. If I tell you to relax, breathe deeply, don't look down, or whatever, the skill wouldn't become any easier. What was an easy skill is now a complex skill, even though the skill itself hasn't changed.

If I were to ask you to stand up in front of a group of people and sing a well-known song, most of you would have a problem, but if I asked the group to sing together, the skill of singing would be much easier.

How many times did I tell my players to practice a skill for a set period and end by saying, "In 10 minutes you will all sit down and then one by one you can show the rest of us how well you have done"? That exercise may be OK for the more talented players, but for those of the group having a problem, the 10 minutes will seem like an hour as they try to master the skill without telling themselves that they will screw up when their turn comes around. Sure enough, the self-fulfilling prophecy says that if you convince yourself that you will fail, you will indeed fail!

What does this have to do with baseball, you may ask. Well, here we are—an 11-year-old in the batter's box, first inning, runner on second, no one out. The coach signals the player to bunt. No problem; he has done it hundreds of times in practice (when the two-by-four is on the ground). Same player, same number of outs, same batter's box, but now the game is the most important game of the year and it's all tied in the bottom of the ninth with one out. How far off the ground is that two-by-four now? No matter how many times he has practiced or how many times he has faced the same situation in other games, this time is different because the bunt is the most important one of this young player's life. He looks at his dad, who gives him the thumbs-up sign. He sees his mom, who has her hands covering her eyes. He sees the rest of the team cheering him on, the opposing team willing him to strike out, his coach telling him to relax and take his time. He hears the coach say, "Don't let the team down!" How high is the two-by-four now, and how narrow has it suddenly become? How can he possibly relax when no one has taught him how to relax? How can he practice positive visualization skills if his coach thinks that all this psychological bunk doesn't help in playing baseball?

When teaching new skills, many coaches try to put the skill under pressure early in the skill-learning continuum. We normally don't introduce pressure training until players have learned the skill to a reasonably high level. In the early stages of the players' skill acquisition, we should keep the level of arousal low because for many athletes, the threat of failure is arousal producing in itself. If the ultimate aim of sport participation at the younger level is fun, then we can put these skills under pressure in a fun activity. For example, if we have 12 players in a 20-yard-by-20-yard grid and 6 of them have a large soft ball, then they can play a game of tag in which they cannot be tagged if they are carrying a ball.

The person who is "it" chases someone who doesn't have a ball. Someone calls out the name of the person being chased and throws him a ball. He is now safe, so the chaser tries to tag someone else. Players may be able to catch a ball 9 times out of 10 when they are standing in straight lines, but in the heat of the chase the pressure may affect not only the catcher but also the thrower. As their skill level improves and the players learn how to handle the pressure, the coach can reduce the number of balls and perhaps increase the size of the grid.

During the early stages, you may want to forget about gloves for a while because some children may still be having difficulty catching a ball with two hands, never mind with the nonpreferred hand.

Mini Olympics Procedure

Another excellent way of increasing the anxiety level and at the same time putting various skills under pressure and introducing some other aspects of the game—namely, agility, balance, power, speed, reaction time, and motor coordination—is what we call a mini Olympics. This chapter came about from my work with one of the best teachers of young players, Chris Johnson, who was born in England and currently lives in Canada. He developed the mini Olympics, which is a fun way to get loosened up.

The mini Olympics concept brings together many aspects of a good coaching model. How many times have we driven past a soccer practice and seen a group of players lined up to dribble one ball between 10 cones or watched a coach hit fly balls to a group of players standing in the field, some of whom are secretly praying the coach won't hit the ball to them because they already know they will drop it? Some statistics show that athletes may be practicing skills only 30 percent of the practice time. The rest of the time is spent standing around waiting for a turn that doesn't last long, setting up and taking down equipment, listening to drawn-out instructions, and so on.

The mini Olympics concept allows a coach to pressurize a series of skills or other aspects of performance in an enjoyable, competitive environment by using the element of time to put the players under pressure. The games can be done indoors or outdoors. A station approach is used. Players in teams of four or five compete against the clock for a set period. The scores are recorded so that a final tally can be made when all teams have completed the total number of stations. The stations should be arranged so that one muscle group is not overworked in two consecutive stations or maximum work output is not required in two consecutive stations, such as maximum sprinting over a short distance followed by speed skipping.

The mini Olympics can also be used just for fun, using activities not necessarily related to the sport. For example, one event could be running to fill a container with water after scooping up water in a large spoon (eye–hand coordination, balance, concentration). The mini Olympics can also be used for purely conditioning activities, preferably with more mature athletes; as a competition among parents; or in a combination of aerobic and anaerobic activities—speed, agility, power, endurance, and fine and gross motor coordination skills.

The design of the stations is up to the creativity and ingenuity of the coach. Athletes can be asked to design stations that emphasizes skill, power, or coordination, or they can develop fun activities such as catching water-filled balloons to develop soft hands.

The coach calls all the players to station 1. While the coach explains what to do, team 1 demonstrates to all the other teams. After the coach is certain that the players all understand, they move to station 2 and team 2 demonstrates, and so on.

After the stations are set up, each team goes to their starting point. On a signal, all the teams try to score as many points as they can within a predetermined time, such as four minutes. If the activities are particularly strenuous, two minutes may be more appropriate.

At the end of the time limit, the coach signals that time is up and calls out the team numbers. The scorer for that team calls out the team's score, and the coach records the score on a score sheet. While this is going on, all the teams move forward one place; team 1 moves to station 2, team 2 moves to station 3, and so on (the highest numbered team moves to station 1). After minimal waiting time, the coach signals the start of the second session. The process continues until the teams complete all stations.

The following example shoes a partially completed final score sheet. At station 1, team 1 scored 20 points, team 2 scored 18 points, team 3 scored 22 points, and so on.

To calculate the final score, we do not just add together all the scores because one team may have substantially outscored all the other teams in just one activity, which could skew the total score. Therefore, we rank the teams according to their scores. For example, in activity A, team 7 scored the most points, 30, and therefore they get 7 points; team 6 scored 28 points, so they get 6 points; and team 5 only scored 16 points, so they get 1 point. In the example, team 1 scored the fourth highest number of points in activity A, the lowest in activity B, and the highest in activity C, and so on, for a total of 28 points (using the fictitious points in activities D, E, F, and G as an example). If two or more teams have the same score, add the points together and divide by the number of teams tied at that score. In the example, teams 2 and 4 both scored 135 points in activity B, placing them in second and third place. They would earn 6 and 5 points, but because they are tied, they get 5 1/2 points each.

In the following examples of the score sheets, you can see how easy it is to move down and across the sheet when writing down the scores. You can print off a few score sheets to streamline the scoring process.

The beauty is that only the coach knows the final tally. Amazingly, many times I have had all teams tie for first place!

The following mini Olympics is for baseball players aged 11 and 12, but it can be modified for any age group, even for the high school and college level.

The following example uses eight stations with 4 or 5 athletes at each station. If you only have 12 athletes, then you need only three stations. The stations are set up in close proximity to each other, enabling the athletes to move quickly from station to station.

When dividing the players into groups, be creative in your method of selecting teams—birthdays, height, first letters of first name, first letter of last name, first letter of mom's or dad's first name. You can draw names out of a hat or have players pick a piece of colored paper out of a bag. For four teams, you would have four different colored slips of paper in a bag and each player would choose one.

Each station should have a counter, preferably a parent, because I like to involve them in practices as much as possible. Otherwise the players do it. When the stations are set up (see later), they are numbered. Team 1 starts at station 1, team 2 at station 2, and so on.

92. Roll Ball and Run

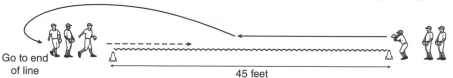

Go to end
of line

45 feet

Purpose

This drill gets the players warmed up, and it works on a few baseball skills—fielding a baseball, catching a baseball with two hands, and running.

Equipment

Two cones

10 softer baseballs or tennis balls

Number of Players

Six

Setup

Place two cones 45 feet apart. Three players are at one cone, and the first has a ball. The other three are at the other cone.

Procedure

1. The first player on the team of three rolls the ball toward the first player opposite him and then sprints to the end of the opposite team.

2. The first player on the other team player runs toward the ball, collects it as it rolls, and then tosses it underhand to the second person on the team that he is running toward.

3. The player who has collected and passed the ball joins the end of his new group and waits to get the ball so that he can roll it and then run to the end of the team where he started.

4. The scoring is one point for every successful catch, two points off for every dropped ball, or however you decide to score it

5. Players are not wearing fielding gloves so they have to use two hands.

Coaching Points

The main point is to make sure that the players do not go too fast and do it correctly.

93. Hot Potato

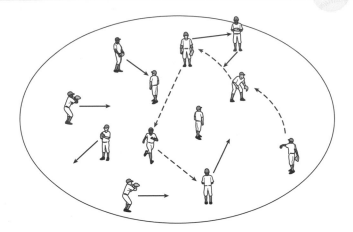

Purpose

To have fun running and tossing the ball to each other. In this drill, the players have to coordinate tossing a baseball as they run, keeping an eye on the other players, and catching it while they are moving. Players have to catch the ball with two hands.

Equipment

Four or five softer balls or tennis balls

Number of Players

6 to 12

Setup

All players in the group are in a 10-yard-by-10-yard grid. Gloves are optional.

Procedure

1. On command, the players run anywhere they can in the grid, throwing to each other as they run. The drill is similar to the game hot potato; the idea is to get rid of the ball as quickly as possible.

2. Count the number of passes, but if the ball is dropped, the counting starts again.

3. The largest number of consecutive passes is what counts at the end.

94. Tag Game

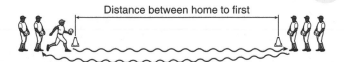

Distance between home to first

Purpose

To work on running to first base and teamwork, as well as tagging a player.

Equipment

Two cones

Six baseballs

Number of Players

Full team

Setup

Place two cones the same distance apart as home plate to first base. Half the team is at one cone, and the other half is at the other cone. Each player has a ball in his throwing hand.

Procedure

1. On the command to go, the first player sprints to the first-base cone and tags the first player at that cone, who then sprints back to the original team, and so on.

2. One point is scored for every tag.

95. Circle

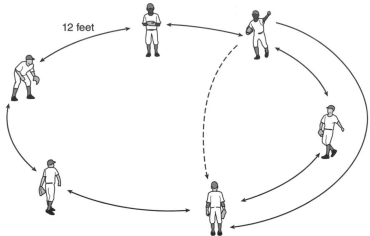

12 feet

Purpose
To work on catching a baseball and running to a certain spot. This is an agility and coordination drill for young kids.

Equipment
Four or five softer baseballs or tennis balls

Number of Players
Six

Setup
Players stand in a circle with approximately 12 feet between players.

Procedure
1. One player starts with a ball, tosses it to another player, and then immediately runs and stands behind that player, who then tosses to someone else and runs to his position.
2. One point is scored for every successful pass.
3. If a player drops the ball, the activity continues after he picks up the ball, but no point is scored.

Coaching Points
- Watch for players tossing the ball correctly and underhand.
- Players should catch the ball with two hands

96. Target

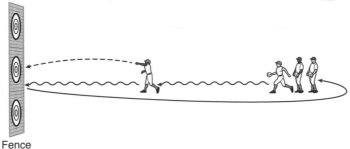

Fence

Purpose
To work on hitting targets, control, and accuracy.

Equipment
At least three targets to hang, which can be Frisbees or colored cardboard squares
Five to 10 tennis balls or softer baseballs

Number of Players
Full team

Setup
Hang a target from the fence behind the plate at about the same height as the batter's hitting zone. You can use three different-sized targets, each with a different point system.

Procedure
1. One player stands by the fence, and the rest of the team stands about 15 yards away behind a cone.
2. The first player identifies his target and throws to it.
3. If it hits, he gets the points.
4. He runs to the fence so that he is ready to retrieve the next pitch, while the player at the fence retrieves the ball, sprints back to the other players, hands the ball to the first in the line, and then goes to the back of the line.

97. Batting Game

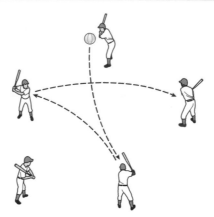

Purpose
The idea is to try to hit the ball while it is in the air.

Equipment
Four or five Wiffle ball bats with very large barrels (tennis racquets can be used instead)

Large soft beach ball

Number of Players
Four or five

Setup
Players, each with a baseball bat, stand in a circle about five yards in diameter. Use a large soft beach ball.

Procedure
1. On the command to start, the player with the ball hits it in the air toward another member of the group, who tries to keep it in the air and hit it to someone else.
2. No player can hit the ball twice consecutively.
3. The score is the most consecutive hits in one rally or the total number of hits within a predetermined time limit.

Coaching Point
*   Keep the players apart from each other and make sure that they do not hit the ball twice in a row.

98. Skip the Rope

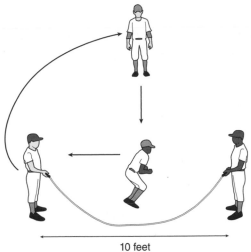

10 feet

Purpose
To work on quick feet, coordination, and teamwork.

Equipment
Jump rope

Number of Players
Four

Setup
Two players hold the ends of a 10-foot skipping rope.

Procedure
1. The players turn the rope, and the next player runs in and does 10 skips.
2. After he has finished, he takes one end of the rope. The next player starts to skip as quickly as possible, and the player who just turned the rope goes to the end of the line.
3. One point is scored per skip.

99. Cone

Purpose

To work on coordination, compete, and have fun.

Equipment

Five cones   Football

Rugby ball

Number of Players

Four

Setup

Place five cones about 3 feet apart in a straight line. Some players line up at the first cone, and others line up at the last cone.

Procedure

1. On the command to go, the first player kicks a football or rugby ball (not a round ball) between the cones to the player at the end, who dribbles it back to the second player on the starting team.
2. The ball must go between all the cones.
3. One point is scored for each successful run.

100. Pickup

Purpose

To work on picking the ball off the ground, agility, coordination, flexibility when going down to get the ball, and teamwork.

Equipment

Baseballs

Four cones

Number of Players

Three to six

Setup

Line up the players behind a cone. Set up another cone 15 feet in front of the first cone. Set up the other cones at 20 feet and 25 feet. Each cone has a baseball beside it.

Procedure

1. On the command to go, the first player runs to pick up a ball at any cone, brings it back to the start cone, and puts it on the ground.

2. The second player runs to pick up another ball and brings it back to the start. The third person brings in the third ball. As soon as he puts it on the ground, the next player picks up a ball and runs to put it by the side of one of the three cones. The next player returns the second ball to a cone, and the third returns the third ball.

3. One point is scored for every ball picked up, whether bringing it in or taking it out. Note that a player cannot start until the player in front of him has returned to the start cone.

Coaching Points

- Because the ball is not rolling, the players should bend their knees to pick up the ball with the throwing hand. They push straight down on top of the baseball to get it.

- Make sure that they push with the hand to get the ball into the ground so that they know they have it.

- Players must go down with both hands so that the shoulders and head follow.

About the Author

Peter Caliendo serves as president of Caliendo Sports International, a global baseball organization specializing in the training of individuals, teams, and coaches, as well as dealing with professional baseball operations worldwide. He recently worked in Japan as a coach alongside Japanese baseball legend and all-time home run champion Sadaharu Ho.

Caliendo studied the development of youth coaching at the legendary Mickey Owen Baseball School as well as the Grand Slam USA, Billy Williams, and Doyle baseball schools. Putting what he learned into practice, he served as the director of the Pan American Youth Baseball Association for six years. During his time with the organization, he oversaw three gold medals and more than 20 players who entered Major League Baseball. He has also served as coach and director for a number of professional teams, including the Belgium Baseball Federation national teams, team USA (where he coached a team in Australia's Intercontinental Cup), the Thunder Bay Whiskey Jacks, and the Schaumburg Flyers. While with the Flyers, Caliendo saw more than 20 players sign with Major League organizations.

Caliendo's resume includes stops at baseball franchises and organizations as a player, coach, and director. He is in his 14th year as a technical commissioner for the International Baseball Federation, where he served as the head of the technical committee for the historic 2009 World Baseball Cup in Europe. In 2012 and 2013 he worked as a technical committee member for the MLB World Baseball Classic's qualifier and first and second rounds in Japan. As a technical commissioner for the International Baseball Federation (IBAF), he served on the jury of appeal for the Olympic Games in Beijing, China, and as a technical commissioner for the Olympic Qualifier in Havana, Cuba. He has served as director for USA Athletes International's Baseball Operations, as an associate scout with the Toronto Blue Jays, as director of baseball operations and coach for the Schaumburg Flyers in the Northern League, and as player procurement director for the North Shore Spirit in the independent Northeast League.

Currently Caliendo serves on the International Baseball Federation's Tournament and Development Committee and is a director of the Great Lakes Region for NTIS—USA Baseball's National Team Identification Program for potential national team players since 2009. He also served as a board member for the Chicago Baseball Museum and as an immediate past president and board member of the Pitch and Hit Club, where he served eight years as president.

Caliendo has produced five instructional baseball DVDs (*Coaching Made Easy*) and has created an online baseball coaches certification program with the Baseball Coaches Video Library in Canada. He has presented at clinics in 20 countries, including the National High School Coaches Baseball Clinic, various High School Association Clinics, and the European Baseball Coaches Association clinic (EBCA). In 2011, Caliendo received both the American Baseball Coaches Association Meritorious Service Award and the Pitch and Hit Club Paul "Dizzy" Trout Ambassador Award and was honored by the Illinois High School Baseball Coaches Association with the Man of the Year award.